BEADS
For All Seasons™

BEADING

D1313662

Beads for All Seasons

From the Editor

In my mind, there's no better way to express my creativity than by making the perfect piece of jewelry to coordinate with a favorite outfit. I frequently wake up a half hour early in the morning so that I can string a necklace to match a floral skirt or a bracelet to go with a new cardigan. I look at it as stress management time—it's my chance to go to work relaxed and refreshed and ready for the day (not to mention well-accessorized).

In the pages of this book you'll find more than 60 projects that are very easy and very fun. Most can be made—start to finish—in a half hour or so. A few will take a little more time, but you'll think they're well worth it when you start receiving compliments about your jewelry!

You'll find projects suitable for wearing with barely-there summer attire and with chunky winter sweaters, with elegant party attire and with casual jeans. This is truly the book of projects for all seasons!

Isn't making our own jewelry wonderful?

Vicki Blizzard

Beads for All Seasons is published by Annie's Attic/DRG Publishing, 306 East Parr Road, Berne, IN 46711, telephone (260) 589-4000. Printed in USA. Copyright © 2005 Annie's Attic/DRG Publishing.

RETAILERS: If you would like to carry this pattern book or any other DRG publications, call the Wholesale Department to set up a direct account: (903) 636-4303. Also, request a complete listing of publications available.

Every effort has been made to ensure that the instructions in this pattern book are complete and accurate. We cannot, however, take responsibility for human error, typographical mistakes or variations in individual work.

Editor: Vicki Blizzard
Associate Editor: Lisa M. Fosnaugh
Art Director: Brad Snow
Assistant Art Director: Nick Pierce
Technical Editor: Brooke Smith
Copy Supervisor: Michelle Beck
Copy Editors: Mary O'Donnell, Beverly Richardson
Graphic Production Supervisor: Ronda Bechinski

ISBN: 1-59635-065-2   Printed in U.S.A.

Graphic Artist: Jessi Butler, Shelley Muhlenkamp
Photography: Tammy Christian, Christena Green, Matthew Owen, Justin P. Wiard, Kelly Wiard
Photo Stylists: Tammy Nussbaum, Tammy M. Smith

Library of Congress Control Number: 2005931540

2 3 4 5 6 7 8 9

Contents

Spring's First Blossom

Design by **Vicki Blizzard**

Beautiful and surprisingly affordable, peridot chips are this season's hottest shade of green. Use the money you save to buy sterling silver beads and findings!

INSTRUCTIONS

Pendant

1) Thread a heishe spacer bead, pink quartz bead and a heishe spacer bead onto sterling silver head pin. Form a wrapped head pin loop, placing a closed jump ring onto loop before wrapping.

Necklace

1) String two crimp beads ½ inch from one end of beading wire; place wire end through end of lobster claw clasp and back through both crimp beads. Use chain-nose pliers to flatten the crimp bead furthest away from clasp.

2) String approximately 1 inch of peridot chips, then string a sterling silver heishe bead; repeat sequence for 9 inches, ending with a silver heishe bead.

3) String pendant onto necklace, then string another silver heishe bead.

4) Repeat step 2 to complete second side of necklace, ending with peridot chips.

5) Repeat step 1, stringing remaining jump ring instead of lobster claw clasp. ●

Source: Beading wire from Beadalon.

MATERIALS

- Peridot chips*
- 20 (4mm) sterling heishe spacer beads
- 10 x 15mm pink quartz rectangular faceted bead
- 4 (1.5mm) silver crimp beads
- 2 (4.7mm) sterling silver closed jump rings
- 25 inches of .015-inch-diameter 49-strand nylon-coated flexible beading wire
- 9mm lobster claw clasp
- 2-inch sterling silver head pin
- Chain-nose pliers
- Wire nippers
- *Model necklace uses approximately half of a 36-inch strand of peridot chips.

FINISHED SIZE

19 inches

Dangling Daisies

Design by **Lisa Galvin**

Nothing is as fresh as a bunch of daisies! Learning to make a daisy chain is quick and easy with this fun project.

MATERIALS

Seed beads: 20 turquoise,
    20 orange and 8 green
2 pearlized white E beads
2 (8mm) green Czech pressed
    glass flower cones
Pair of silver French ear wires
2 (17-inch) lengths white nylon
    bead-stringing thread
Fine collapsible eye
    beading needle
Small scissors

FINISHED SIZE

1⁷⁄₈ inches long

INSTRUCTIONS

1) Insert one end of a 17-inch length of thread through loop on ear wire; bring thread ends together to make thread even. Tie a small knot next to ear-wire loop to secure thread. Insert thread ends onto beading needle.

2) Slide 10 turquoise seed beads on beading needle; slide on six orange seed beads and one pearlized white E bead. Push all beads close to ear-wire loop.

3) Referring to Fig. 1, insert needle back through first orange seed bead and pull taut; string on four additional orange seed beads. Referring to Fig. 2, insert needle through the bottom orange seed bead to form a flower. String on three green seed beads and flower cone. Remove beading needle from thread.

4) Separate doubled thread and slide a green seed bead on only one of the threads, pushing it to the bottom of the flower cone. Bring thread ends together and tie a knot close to seed bead.

5) Slip loose thread ends back on beading needle; insert beading needle up through flower cone and green seed beads. Pull excess thread taut; trim thread close to green seed beads to conceal.

6) Repeat steps 1–5 for second earring. ●

Source: Bead stringing thread from Beadalon.

Fig. 1   Fig. 2

Delicate Dangles

Design by **Lisa Galvin**

Just add a pendant and a few beads to suede lace for an easy, stylish lariat. You can make it in minutes!

INSTRUCTIONS

1) Thread one lace end through a barrel bead and a 10mm jump ring; thread lace end back through barrel bead using an embroidery needle to help pull lace through.

2) Add a small dot of adhesive between leather layers at top of barrel bead before cinching jump ring to secure. Pull lace lightly to cinch, holding jump ring in place. Trim excess lace end close to barrel bead.

3) Repeat steps 1 and 2 for opposite end of lace.

4) Attach pendant to jump ring on one end of lariat.

5) For opposite end of lariat, thread crystallized bead on an eye pin; use round-nose pliers to form a loop at top of bead. Trim excess wire. Attach loop to jump ring on lariat. Use a 5mm jump ring to attach heart clasp to bottom loop on eye pin. Use remaining 5mm jump ring to attach leaf charm to the jump ring on lariat. ●

Sources: Pendant from Expo International Inc.; embossed beads from The Beadery; jewel adhesive from Beacon.

MATERIALS

- 25mm amethyst heart pendant
- 2 (⅝-inch-long) Peruvian barrel-shaped embossed beads
- Silver heart-shaped leaf charm
- 20mm clear crystallized glass bead
- Silver heart-shaped clasp end
- Silver jump rings: 2 (10mm), 2 (5mm)
- 1-inch silver eye pin
- 36 inches ⅛-inch-wide black suede lace
- Embroidery needle
- Round-nose pliers
- Chain-nose pliers
- Wire nippers
- Gem adhesive

FINISHED SIZE

36 inches

Pink Perfection

Design by **Katie Hacker**

Ribbon watches are everywhere this season.
Use double-sided ribbon and a large watch
face for a dramatic fashion statement.

MATERIALS

Silver watch face with
  horizontal top and
  bottom pins
24 inches pink satin
  double-sided ribbon
8 (6mm) clear AB faceted
  bicone beads
8 (1mm) silver head pins
Round-nose pliers
Chain-nose pliers
Wire nippers
Permanent fabric adhesive

FINISHED SIZE
Will fit all wrist sizes

INSTRUCTIONS

1) Cut each end of ribbon diagonally; apply a small amount of fabric adhesive to ends to prevent fraying. Let dry.

2) String a bicone bead on a head pin; use the widest part of the round-nose pliers to form a large loop above bead. Trim excess wire and attach loop to the upper left side of watch face. Use chain-nose pliers to secure loop closed.

3) String each remaining bicone bead on a head pin; use the smallest part of the round-nose pliers to form a loop above each bead. Trim excess wires and attach each beaded head pin to the first beaded head pin loop already in place on watch face.

4) Thread ribbon through watch face. To wear, tie ribbon in a bow or knot around wrist. ●

Sources: Watch face from Fire Mountain Gems & Beads; beads and head pins from Beadalon; fabric adhesive from Beacon.

Jeweled Scatter Pins

Designs by **Katie Hacker**

Attach a few beaded head pins below an upside-down pendant to create these chic, easy accessories.

MATERIALS

Small flower and rhinestone
   pendant
Assorted seed, E and tube
   beads in matching colors
3 (1½-inch-long) silver
   head pins
Silver tie-tack pin back
Round-nose pliers
Chain-nose pliers
Wire nippers
Metal adhesive

FINISHED SIZE

Approximately ¾ x 1½ inches

INSTRUCTIONS

1) String an assortment of beads on a head pin for approximately ¾ inch; use round-nose pliers to form a loop above top bead. Trim excess wire and attach loop to pendant loop. Secure loop closed with chain-nose pliers.

2) In same manner as in step 1, string an assortment of beads on a head pin for approximately ½ inch. Form a loop above top bead. Trim excess wire and attach head pin to pendant loop. Repeat once.

3) Glue a tie-tack pin on back of pendant; let dry. ●

Sources: Pendant and beads from Blue Moon Beads; tie-tack pin back from Westrim Crafts; metal adhesive from Beacon.

Pastel Hearts

Design by **Margot Potter**

Beaded chains are very popular for bracelets—
try beading short lengths of fine chain to create
swingy earrings to coordinate.

INSTRUCTIONS

1) Remove metal bead from bottom of extension chain by cutting link above bead with flush cutters.
Attach a jump ring at bottom of chain and slide on heart charm; close jump ring.

2) Slide a corrugated rondelle onto an open jump ring; place it onto a bottom link on the left side of the
chain, securing it closed with chain-nose pliers. Repeat for right side of chain.

3) Repeat step 2, adding beads along length of extension chain in following sequence: green, topaz brown,
pink, corrugated rondelles, green, topaz brown and pink.

4) Remove excess chain by cutting the link above last set of pony beads. Use a jump ring to attach top of
chain to earring post.

5) Repeat steps 1–4 for second earring. ●

Source: Extension chains from Beadalon; heart charms, star earring findings and pony beads from Blue Moon Beads.

MATERIALS

- 8 (5mm) silver-plated
  corrugated rondelles
- Pony beads: 8 green, 8 pink and
  8 topaz brown
- 2 silver-plated filigree
  heart charms
- 36 (4mm) sterling silver
  jump rings
- 2 (1¼-inch) lengths silver-
  plated extension chains
- 2 silver-plated 5-point star
  earring posts with clutches
- Round-nose pliers
- Chain-nose pliers
- Flush cutters

FINISHED SIZE

2 inches long

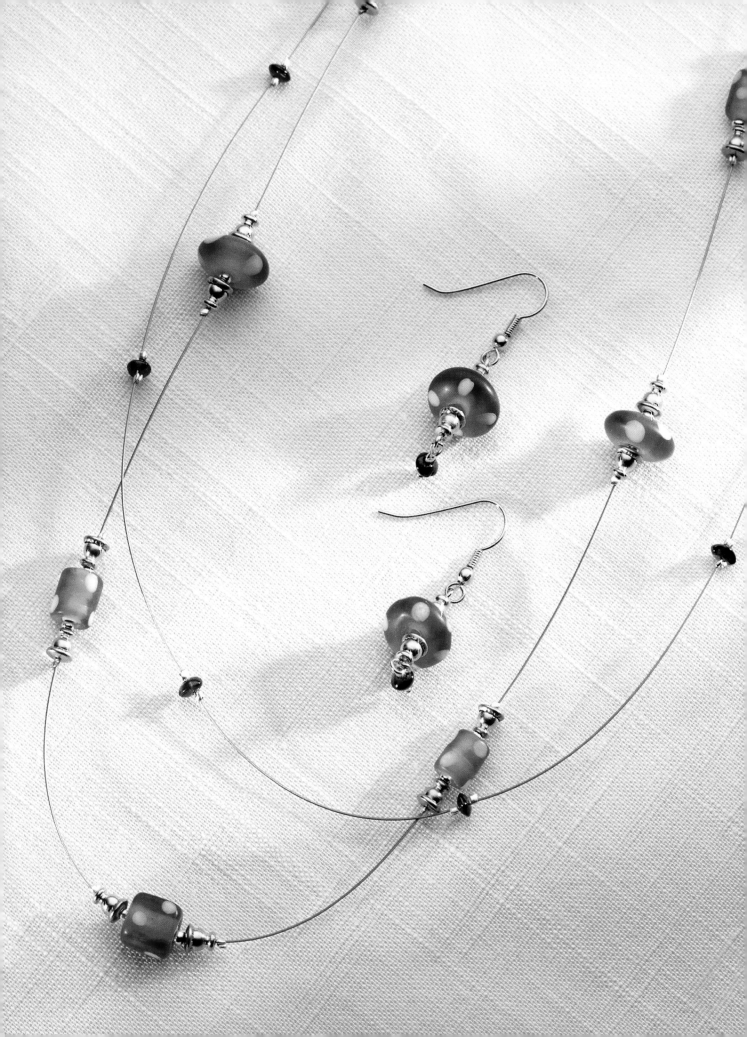

Polka Dots on Parade

Designs by **Lisa Galvin**

Tiny crimp beads add a little shimmer to this polka dot duo. The interesting metallic beads are really earring backs!

INSTRUCTIONS

Necklace

1) Cut two 26-inch lengths of beading wire. String two crimp beads onto one wire approximately ½ inch from end; thread wire end through a hole on one end of the filigree clasp and back through crimp beads. Use crimp tool to flatten crimp beads.

2) String beads onto wire in following order: crimp bead, earring back, silver seed bead, polka-dot bead, silver seed bead, earring back and a crimp bead. Repeat this sequence eight times, alternating the direction of the earring backs.

3) String two additional crimp beads onto wire approximately ½ inch from end. Thread wire end through one hole in remaining end of filigree clasp and back through crimp beads. Flatten crimp beads.

4) Referring to photo and beginning with the center set, use a bead board to adjust beads so that sets are approximately 1½ to 2 inches apart. *Note: Each set will have a crimp bead on each end. Flatten crimp beads next to earring backs to hold beads in place.*

5) Connect second 26-inch length of wire to remaining hole in one end of filigree clasp in same manner as in step 1. String a crimp bead, garnet button bead and another crimp bead onto wire; repeat sequence nine more times.

6) String two additional crimp beads onto wire approximately ½ inch from end. Attach wire to remaining end of clasp in same manner as in step 3.

7) Referring to photo, adjust bead sets so they align between the polka-dot bead sets on other wire. Flatten crimp beads to secure placement of each set.

Earrings

1) Onto a gold eye pin, slide an earring back, polka-dot bead and another earring back. Use round-nose pliers to form a loop above earring back; attach to ear wire and trim wire end.

2) Onto a silver eye pin, slide a crimp bead, garnet button bead and another crimp bead. Flatten crimp beads to hold garnet in place. Form a loop above crimp bead; attach to bottom of beaded gold eye pin and trim wire end.

3) Repeat steps 1 and 2 for remaining ear wire. ●

Source: Beading wire, filigree clasp, crimp beads, eye and head pins from Beadalon; polka-dot beads from The Beadery; garnet button beads from Blue Moon Beads.

MATERIALS

- Pink glass polka-dot beads
- Garnet button beads
- Silver seed beads
- 50 (1.3mm) silver crimp beads
- 22 gold-tone bullet-style earring backs
- 2 gold 1-inch-long eye pins
- 2 silver ½-inch-long head pins
- .015-inch-diameter 19-strand bronze beading wire
- Gold 2-strand filigree clasp
- 2 gold ear wires
- Wire nippers
- Round-nose pliers
- Crimp pliers

FINISHED SIZES

Necklace
   25 inches

Earrings
   1¾ inches long

Shimmering Pearls

Design by **Vicki Blizzard**

Three delicate strands add up to one powerful punch in this freshwater pearl necklace. Wear it often—it is as comfortable and pretty with jeans and a white shirt as it is with a little black dress or a power suit!

INSTRUCTIONS

Strand 1

1) Cut a 22-inch length of beading wire. String two crimp beads ½ inch from end of beading wire; thread wire end through first jump ring on clasp and back through both crimp beads. Gently squeeze crimp bead furthest away from jump ring and fold in half with crimp pliers.

2) String on a seed bead, a small rice pearl, a large rice pearl, a daisy spacer, a potato pearl, a daisy spacer, a large rice pearl and a small rice pearl. Repeat beading sequence 12 additional times. String on one additional seed bead.

3) String on two crimp beads and thread wire end through second jump ring on clasp and back through both crimp beads. Gently squeeze and fold crimp bead furthest from jump ring in half. Trim excess wire.

Strand 2

1) Cut a 22-inch length of beading wire. String two crimp beads and seven seed beads ½ inch from end of beading wire; thread wire end through jump ring on clasp and back through crimp beads and seed beads. Tug wire gently until loop closes around jump ring. Gently squeeze crimp bead furthest away from jump ring and fold in half with crimp pliers.

2) String a large rice pearl, a daisy spacer, a large rice pearl, a daisy spacer, a large rice pearl and seven seed beads. Repeat beading sequence 13 additional times.

3) Repeat step 3 of Strand 1, pulling wire through crimp beads and seven seed beads before closing crimp bead.

MATERIALS

- 13 (8mm) freshwater potato pearls
- 68 (8mm) and 80 (6mm) freshwater rice pearls
- 340 sea green iridescent Delica seed beads
- 70 (4mm) sterling silver daisy spacers
- 1-inch sterling silver S clasp with attached jump rings
- 12 silver crimp beads
- 66 inches .015-inch-diameter 49-strand nylon-coated flexible beading wire
- Crimp pliers
- Wire nippers

FINISHED SIZE

19¼ inches including clasp

CONTINUED ON PAGE 125

Bubbly Brooch

Design by **Mary Lynn Maloney**

Transform a plain bottle cap into an imaginative, personalized brooch. Use dimensional adhesive to fill the inside of the cap, then add an initial and some playful wire and beads. Pin your creation onto a jacket, purse or backpack.

MATERIALS

Bottle cap

Mini bottle cap initial

Pastel striped paper

22-gauge turquoise and
    purple wire

5 silver spacer beads in
    assorted shapes

6 to 8 glass beads in assorted
    shapes and sizes

Pink felt

Tie-tack pin

Round-nose pliers

Hammer

Metal adhesive

Fabric adhesive

Clear dimensional adhesive

FINISHED SIZE

3 inches

INSTRUCTIONS

1) Pound the back of the bottle cap with a hammer to slightly fan out the rippled edge of cap.

2) Cut pastel paper to fit inside bottle cap; glue paper inside cap with dimensional adhesive. Apply a generous, even layer of dimensional adhesive on top of striped paper; let dry. Use metal adhesive to glue mini bottle cap initial inside cap.

3) Wrap turquoise and purple wires around bottle cap randomly; twist ends together on back to secure.

4) Fold a 10-inch length of purple wire in half and attach to the twisted wire on back, letting purple wire ends extend below bottle cap. Repeat with a 3-inch length of turquoise wire.

5) Cut a circle from felt to fit onto the reverse side of bottle cap to cover wires; adhere with fabric adhesive.

6) Thread spacer and glass beads onto wire ends below cap. Secure beads by randomly twisting and curling wires.

7) Use metal adhesive to attach tie-tack pin to back of cap. ●

Sources: Bottle caps from Li'l Davis Designs; wire from Artistic Wire; dimensional adhesive from JudiKins; Glass, Metal & More and Fabri-Tac adhesives from Beacon.

New Mom Charm Bracelet

Design by **Samantha McNesby**

This pretty bracelet would make an appreciated shower gift for a new mother-to-be!

INSTRUCTIONS

1) Place a pink bead on a head pin; use needle-nose pliers to create a loop at top of bead and snip away excess. Repeat for all pink and blue beads.

2) Place one silver spacer, crystal bead and another silver spacer onto a head pin. Create a loop at top of spacer; snip away excess and repeat for remaining crystal bead and silver spacers.

3) Using needle-nose pliers, open a ¼-inch jump ring and place the "ABC" blocks onto it; close jump ring.

4) Open remaining ¼-inch jump ring and place baby spoon and baby cup charms onto it; close jump ring.

5) Use ⅛-inch jump rings to attach charms to bracelet; leave two to three links between each charm, depending on size of charm. Place charms on bracelet in the following order: flat pink oval, baby shoe, crystal diamond, baby cup and spoon, frosted blue round, teddy bear, pink rectangle, blocks, crystal cube, baby carriage and flat blue oval. ●

MATERIALS

- 7½-inch silver link bracelet
- Silver charms:
  - teddy bear
  - baby carriage
  - baby cup
  - baby spoon
  - baby shoe
  - 3 "ABC" blocks
- Glass and crystal beads:
  - clear crystal cube
  - clear crystal diamond
  - flat blue oval
  - flat pink oval
  - frosted blue round
  - frosted pink rectangle
- 4 (⅛-inch) silver spacers
- 2 (¼-inch) silver jump rings
- 11 (⅛-inch) silver jump rings
- 6 silver head pins
- Needle-nose pliers
- Wire nippers

FINISHED SIZE

7½ inches

Blooming Blossoms

Designs by **Jennifer Mayer Fish**

Pins are this year's hot fashion accessory. Make a small, simple flower to wear at the office or a big, bold blossom for a night on the town.

INSTRUCTIONS

1) Cut an 18-inch length of wire. Thread one oblong bead 4 inches from wire end; bend and wrap long wire end around base of bead several times to secure bead to wire. Leave 4-inch wire as is.

2) String another oblong bead onto the long portion of wire; bend and wrap wire around itself at base of bead, positioning bead so it is next to the first bead.

3) Repeat step 2 until there are four beads on wire, positioning beads in a flower shape.

4) String fifth oblong bead on long portion of wire. Thread the 4-inch wire end left from step 1, through fifth bead. Bend and twist wires around each other to secure final oblong bead.

5) Wrap excess wire around the other beads, securing beads together. Trim excess wire.

6) Cut an 8-inch length of wire; string on round bead, positioning bead so it is on the center of the wire. Place the bead onto the center of the flower; pull wire ends through to the reverse side of the flower and twist them together to secure.

7) Attach the flower to pin back by wrapping the wire ends around the flat portion of pin several times; trim excess wire. For extra security, apply a small amount of bead glue to reverse side of flower to secure it to pin back. ●

Sources: Beads from Cousin Corp. of America, Darice, Blue Moon Beads and Westrim Crafts; Aleene's Glass & Bead Glue from Duncan.

MATERIALS

- 5 oblong beads in desired color, at least ⅜ inch long for flower petals
- Round bead for flower center
- Silver pin back
- 22-gauge silver wire
- Wire nippers
- Bead glue

FINISHED SIZE

Ranges in size from 1⅜ to 2¼ inches, depending on size of beads used

Intertwining Neutrals

Design by **Vicki Blizzard**

Pearlized seed beads dance and twist among natural mother-of-pearl beads. Touches of gold add a little formality to this whimsical necklace!

Project note: Mother-of-pearl beads have an opaque white spot at one end. String beads with the white ends all facing in the same direction.

INSTRUCTIONS

1) Cut a 24-inch piece of beading wire. String two crimp beads ½ inch from end of beading wire; place wire end through bar end of toggle and back through both crimp beads. Gently squeeze crimp bead furthest away from clasp in half with crimp pliers.

2) Alternate stringing a mother-of-pearl bead and a gold crimp tube, ending with a mother-of-pearl bead.

3) Repeat step 1, stringing remaining end of toggle clasp instead of bar end.

4) Repeat step 1 with remaining length of beading wire.

5) String 25 inches of seed beads. Twist seed bead strand around mother-of-pearl strand.

6) Repeat step 3. ●

Source: Beading wire from Beadalon.

MATERIALS

- 46 (8mm) natural (unbleached) round mother-of-pearl beads
- 53 (2mm) gold crimp tubes
- Light tan pearlized seed beads
- Gold vermeil toggle clasp
- 54 inches .015-inch-diameter 49-strand nylon-coated flexible beading wire
- Crimp pliers
- Wire nippers

FINISHED SIZE

- 21 inches

Faux-Pearl Swirl

Design by **Katherine McBee**

Faux pearls and satin cord twist around memory wire creating a delicate bridal choker. Be creative and string a similar design on smaller memory wire to make coordinating a hair accessory.

Project note: Memory wire is hard to cut and will damage regular wire nippers. Always use heavy-duty wire cutters or memory wire shears to cut wire coils.

INSTRUCTIONS

1) Use round-nose pliers to form a loop at one end of memory wire. Beginning with a crystal bead, slide crystal beads and bugle beads onto memory wire, alternating crystal beads and bugles. Repeat until end of memory wire is reached. Form a loop at the wire end.

2) Cut a 36-inch length of 28-gauge silver wire; form a small loop at one end of wire. String on two seed beads.

3) String on one 4mm pearl and a seed bead; repeat 16 additional times.

4) String on an 8mm pearl, a seed bead, a 4mm pearl and a seed bead. Repeat this sequence 43 additional times.

5) Repeat step 3, only in reverse. String on two seed beads. Form a small loop at end of wire.

6) Beginning approximately 4 inches from one end of memory wire, wrap ¼ inch of one end of beaded silver wire securely around the memory wire; referring to photo, continue to wrap beaded wire around memory wire. Secure wire end around memory wire approximately 4 inches from end of memory wire.

7) Cut 31 inches of satin cord. Secure one end of cord at one end of memory wire by tying a knot next to the first bead. Referring to photo, wrap cord around entire length of memory wire, positioning cord between beaded silver wire. Tie a knot at the end; trim ends if needed and secure with glue.

8) Slide a 4mm pearl onto a head pin; form a loop at top and attach to one end of beaded memory wire. Repeat for remaining end of memory wire.

9) Cut two 5-inch pieces of silver wire. Form a loop at one end on each piece. String 25 (4mm) pearls onto each wire. Form another loop at each wire end. Wrap beaded wires around each end of beaded memory wire. ●

Source: Bugle beads and crystal beads from Nicole Crafts.

MATERIALS

- 8mm and 4mm white pearls
- 8/0 opaque multicolored glass seed beads
- 4mm clear crystal beads
- ¼-inch-long clear bugle beads
- 2 silver head pins
- 17½ inches necklace memory wire
- 46 inches 28-gauge silver wire
- 31 inches white satin cord
- Round-nose pliers
- Heavy-duty wire cutters
- Jeweler's glue

FINISHED SIZE

Necklace can be adjusted to fit most neck sizes

Chunky Treasures

Design by **Vicki Blizzard**

Chunky beads are made flexible with the addition of daisy and cube spacers in between. Wrap your wrist in this treasure of pale green aventurine and prepare for compliments!

INSTRUCTIONS

1) String two crimp beads ½ inch from end of beading wire; place wire end through jump ring attached to clasp and thread back through crimp beads. Use chain-nose pliers to flatten crimp bead furthest away from clasp.

2) String a cube bead, a daisy spacer, a nugget and a daisy spacer. Repeat seven more times. String a cube bead.

3) String two crimp beads and other end of clasp. Thread end of wire back through crimp beads and several other beads. Use chain-nose pliers to flatten crimp bead furthest away from jump ring. Trim excess wire. ●

Sources: Nugget beads from Fire Mountain Gems & Beads; cube beads, Bali spacers and toggle clasp from Enchanting Beads; beading wire from Beadalon.

MATERIALS

- 8 (approximately 12mm x 18mm) pale green aventurine nugget beads
- 9 (2.5mm) silver cube beads
- 16 (3mm) Bali daisy spacers
- 4 silver crimp beads
- Silver toggle clasp with chain extension
- 14 inches .015-inch-diameter 49-strand nylon-coated flexible beading wire
- Chain-nose pliers
- Wire nippers

FINISHED SIZE

8½ inches

Pretty in Pastel

Design by **Katie Hacker** for Beadalon

Wear this adjustable chain belt over a tunic shirt or through the belt loops of your favorite pair of broken-in jeans. If you're feeling really adventurous, wear it as a tassel necklace. The S-hook allows for all sorts of style options!

Designer tip: *To wear the belt, wrap it loosely around your hips. Fasten the clasp end above the beaded section.*

MATERIALS

Silver medium cable chain

Clear glass leaf beads with front-to-back holes: 4 (12mm) and 6 (10mm)

Glass beads: 3 (8mm) faceted pink, 3 (8mm) faceted green, 3 (8mm) fluted blue, 5 (6mm) round purple and 3 (12mm) rectangular multicolored

Silver hook clasp

10 (6mm) silver jump rings

1 (4mm) silver jump ring

17 (1-inch) silver head pins

Round-nose pliers

Chain-nose pliers

Wire nippers

INSTRUCTIONS

1) Drape the chain loosely around your hips. Add 6 inches and cut the chain to that length. Use a 4mm jump ring and round-nose pliers to attach the clasp to one end of the chain.

2) String each leaf onto a jump ring. Attach the jump rings evenly spaced onto the last 6 inches of the chain on the opposite end from the clasp.

3) String each bead onto a head pin. Form a loop above each bead and cut off excess wire. Attach the beads evenly spaced on the last 6 inches of the chain. ●

Sources: Chain, clasp, jump rings, head pins, round-nose pliers, chain-nose pliers and wire cutters from Beadalon; beads from Blue Moon Beads.

Crimp & Go

Design by **Lisa Galvin**

Add a touch of sparkle and shine to any outfit with dainty glass beads skipping across beading wire.

MATERIALS

28 inches silver 19-strand
    flexible beading wire
26 (4mm) green faceted
    glass beads
12 (4mm x 5mm) barrel
    spacer beads
28 (1.3mm) silver crimp beads
Silver hook and eye clasp
Crimping pliers
Flush-cut wire cutters
Ruler

FINISHED SIZE

21½ inches

INSTRUCTIONS

1) String a crimp bead and one half of clasp onto wire; insert wire end back through crimp bead, leaving a short wire tail.

2) Crimp the crimp bead to secure clasp.

3) String on a faceted glass bead and another crimp bead; crimp the crimp bead and cut excess wire.

4) Measure 1 inch from end of first bead set; string on a crimp bead and crimp. String on a faceted glass bead, barrel spacer, faceted glass bead and another crimp bead. Crimp the second crimp bead.

5) Repeat step 4 eleven times.

6) Measure 1 inch from last bead set and string a crimp bead, faceted glass bead, crimp bead and remaining half of clasp; insert wire end back through bead set and crimp both crimp beads. Cut excess wire. ●

Source: Wire, hook and eye clasp and crimp beads from Beadalon.

Steel Garden

Design by **Margot Potter**

Delicate butterflies flutter over metal daisy beads. Wear these earrings when you're celebrating warm weather and sunny skies.

MATERIALS

2 silver-plated butterfly beads

6 silver-plated small
    flower beads

2mm faceted Czech glass oval
    beads: 2 mint green, 2 light
    blue and 2 silver

Small cable chain: 2 (⅞-inch)
    lengths, 2 (1¼-inch)
    lengths and 2 (1½-inch)
    lengths

2 sterling silver jump rings

6 (24-gauge) 1½-inch-long
    sterling silver head pins

2 (24-gauge) 1½-inch-long
    sterling silver eye pins

2 sterling silver ball hook
    French ear wires

Round-nose pliers

Chain-nose pliers

Flush cutters

FINISHED SIZE

2¾ inches long

INSTRUCTIONS

1) Slide a metal butterfly bead onto an eye pin; use round-nose pliers to form a wrapped head pin loop above bead, attaching to ear wire before wrapping. Trim excess wire.

2) Attach a jump ring to bottom loop on butterfly.

3) Slide a green bead and a flower bead onto a head pin; form a loop above flower bead and attach to the bottom of one of the shortest pieces of chain in same manner as in step 1.

4) Repeat step 3 twice using a blue bead and a silver bead; attach blue bead to medium-length chain and silver bead to longest-length chain.

5) Attach chains to jump ring on butterfly.

6) Repeat steps 1–5 for second ear wire. ●

Sources: Cable chain from Beadalon; flower and butterfly beads from Great Craft Works.

Crystal Craze

Designs by **Katie Hacker**

Cast metal "slider" beads are lovely when paired with crystal bicones.

INSTRUCTIONS

Green Earrings

1) String the following beads onto a 2-inch head pin: bicone green crystal, 12mm green metal bead and another bicone green crystal.

2) Use round-nose pliers to form a loop above top bead; trim off excess wire. Attach the loop to an ear wire; close loop.

3) Repeat steps 1 and 2 for second earring.

Blue Earrings

1) Fold one 3-inch length of wire in half; thread the ends through the holes on the rectangular blue crystal slide.

2) Use round-nose pliers to form one wire end into a loop approximately ⅛ inch above the crystal slide. Slide the ear wire onto the loop, then wrap the extra wire around the base of the loop, catching the other wire end. Trim excess wire.

3) String a blue crystal bead onto a 1-inch-long head pin. Form a loop above bead and attach to wire below crystal slide; close loop and trim excess wire.

4) Repeat steps 1–3 for second earring.

Purple Earrings

1) Fold a 4-inch piece of wire in half; thread ends through the holes on the purple crystal slide.

2) String a purple crystal bead onto each wire end. Use round-nose pliers to form a loop on each wire end; turn loops to form spirals. The spirals should hold the beads in place just below the slide.

3) Attach an ear wire to the wire above the crystal slide.

4) Repeat steps 1–3 for second earring. ●

Source: Swarovski crystal metal sliders and beads from Pure Allure; wire from Beadalon.

MATERIALS

- 2 (12mm) round green metal beads with green crystal inset
- 2 (15mm) rectangular metal slides with blue crystal inset
- 2 (15mm) metal slides with purple crystal inset
- 4 (5mm) bicone green crystal beads
- 2 (4mm) bicone blue crystal beads
- 4 (4mm) bicone purple crystal beads
- 2 (4-inch) lengths 20-gauge silver wire
- 2 (3-inch) lengths 20-gauge silver wire
- Silver 1- and 2-inch-long head pins
- Silver ear wires
- Round-nose pliers
- Chain-nose pliers
- Wire cutters

FINISHED SIZE

Approximately 1½ inches long

Juicy Fruit

Design by **Margot Potter**

With summertime sparkle in vibrant sun-drenched colors, these post-and-dangle earrings have lots of movement and add a little sass and sizzle to warm-weather fashion.

MATERIALS

2 (8mm) yellow and 6 (4mm) pale green AB Swarovski crystal bicone beads

2 orange striated crackled faceted Chinese glass rectangles

4 silver jump rings

4 (22-gauge) and 6 (24-gauge) sterling silver head pins

2 silver coil earring posts

2 rubber earring stoppers

Round-nose pliers

Chain-nose pliers

Flush-cut wire cutters

FINISHED SIZE

2¼ inches long

INSTRUCTIONS

1) Slide a yellow bicone bead on a 22-gauge head pin; cut off head part of head pin. Use round-nose pliers to form a loop at each end of bead. Trim excess wire.

2) Repeat step 1 with an orange glass rectangle.

3) Slide a pale green bicone bead on a 24-gauge head pin; form a wrapped head pin loop above bead, attaching loop to a jump ring before wrapping. Repeat twice.

4) Attach beaded jump rings to one loop on orange glass rectangle. Secure jump rings closed with chain-nose pliers.

5) Attach the top of the orange glass rectangle to one end of yellow bicone bead. Attach a jump ring to remaining end of yellow bicone bead. Attach jump ring to earring post. Secure ring closed with chain-nose pliers.

6) Repeat steps 1–5 for second earring. ●

Sources: Jump rings from Beadalon; Chinese glass rectangles from Phoenix Jewelry & Parts Inc.; coil earring posts from Blue Moon Beads.

Miami Beach

Design by **Margot Potter**

Threader earrings are super hot in the world of jewelry. These simple linear drops can also be made using regular chain and French wires for a similar effect.

INSTRUCTIONS

1) Slide a faceted pearl on a head pin; use round-nose pliers to form a wrapped head pin loop above pearl, attaching loop to jump ring on earring thread before wrapping. Trim excess wire.

2) Repeat step 1 with olive green cube bead.

3) Repeat step 1 with yellow glass bead.

4) Repeat steps 1–3 for second earring. ●

Sources: Pearls from Thunderbird Supply Co.; threader earring components from Rings & Things.

MATERIALS

- 2 (6mm) faceted orange pearls
- 2 (6mm) diagonal-drilled Swarvoski crystal olive green cube beads
- 2 (8mm) yellow AB faceted Czech glass beads
- 6 (22-gauge) sterling silver head pins
- Pair of 5-inch threader earring components with jump ring ends
- Round-nose pliers
- Chain-nose pliers
- Flush-cut wire cutters

FINISHED SIZE

Entire earring is 5¼ inches long

Something's Fishy

Design by **Margot Potter**

MATERIALS

Orange and red Czech glass
    fish beads

2 striated green/clear Czech
    glass windowpane beads

4 gold medium toggle
    clasp circles

4 gold jump rings

4 gold head pins

Pair of gold French ear wires

Round-nose pliers

Chain-nose pliers

Wire nippers

FINISHED SIZE

2¾ inches long

Funky fish combine with two-tone glass windowpane beads and gold-plated toggle circles for an elegant design with a twist.

INSTRUCTIONS

1) Place a fish bead on a head pin; use round-nose pliers to form a loop above bead. Trim excess wire. Repeat with a windowpane bead. Attach both beaded head pins to a jump ring.

2) Open jump ring and attach it to one of the gold toggle circles; use chain-nose pliers to secure jump ring closed.

3) Attach another jump ring to the top of the gold toggle circle; attach jump ring to the bottom of another gold toggle circle. Attach gold toggle circle to loop at bottom of ear wire.

4) Repeat steps 1–3 for second earring. ●

Sources: Fish beads from Great Craft Works; toggles, jump rings and ear wires from Beadalon.

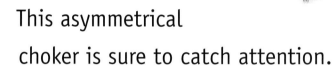

Color Splash

Design by **Lisa Galvin**

This asymmetrical choker is sure to catch attention. Suspend brightly colored, wire-wrapped baubles between chunky, blue, silver-lined beads for a fresh look.

Project notes: Memory wire is hard to cut and will damage regular wire nippers. Always use heavy-duty wire cutters or memory-wire shears to cut wire coils. If holes are large and cause the beads to move too much on memory wire, fill the hole with a piece of rubber tubing that is equal in diameter to the hole.

INSTRUCTIONS

1) Following manufacturer's instructions, apply 2-part epoxy to one end of memory wire; attach memory wire end cap. Let glue set for several hours before proceeding.

2) Cut five ³⁄₁₆-inch pieces and two 5¾-inch pieces of rubber tubing. Slide one 5¾-inch piece on memory wire.

3) String the following on memory wire: E bead, spool spacer, wire-wrapped bead, spool spacer, ³⁄₁₆-inch piece of rubber tubing, blue bead, E bead, ³⁄₁₆-inch piece of rubber tubing, spool spacer, wire-wrapped bead, spool spacer, ³⁄₁₆-inch piece of rubber tubing, spool spacer, wire-wrapped bead, spool spacer, ³⁄₁₆-inch piece of rubber tubing, E bead, blue bead, E bead, ³⁄₁₆-inch piece of rubber tubing, spool spacer, wire-wrapped bead, spool spacer and E bead.

4) Slide on remaining 5¾-inch piece of rubber tubing.

5) Apply 2-part epoxy to wire end and attach an end cap. Let glue set several hours. ●

Sources: Memory wire, memory wire end caps, rubber tubing and 2-part epoxy from Beadalon; beads from Halcraft USA Inc.

MATERIALS

- 4 brightly colored wire-wrapped beads
- 2 blue silver-lined beads
- 8 silver spool-shaped spacer beads
- 5 clear E beads
- 1½ continuous loops necklace memory wire
- 14 inches 2.5mm black rubber tubing
- 2 (5mm) silver round memory wire end caps
- Heavy-duty wire cutters
- 2-part epoxy adhesive

FINISHED SIZES

Can be adjusted to fit most necks

Pearls & Filigree

Design by **Jennifer Mayer Fish**

MATERIALS

Pearls: 6 (4mm) white, 4 (6mm)
   light green and 2 (8mm)
   light green
2 (4mm) green E beads
6 green seed beads
2 (6mm) clear crystal
   rhinestones
2 silver decorative earring
   findings with flat
   center area
4 (4mm) and 6 (6mm) silver
   jump rings
6 silver head pins
Pair of silver French ear wires
Round-nose pliers
Chain-nose pliers
Wire nippers
Gem adhesive

FINISHED SIZE

2⅝ inches long

Delicate pearls and rhinestones swirl and dance for a look that's undeniably vintage.

INSTRUCTIONS

1) String a seed bead, an 8mm light green pearl, an E bead and a 4mm white pearl on a head pin; use round-nose pliers to form a loop above top pearl. Trim excess wire. Attach loop to a 6mm jump ring and attach jump ring to center bottom of silver earring finding. Close jump ring with chain-nose pliers.

2) String a 4mm white pearl, a seed bead and a 6mm light green pearl on a head pin; form a loop above top pearl. Trim excess wire. Repeat to make another beaded head pin. Attach 6mm jump rings to both beaded head pins and attach one to each side loop of earring finding.

3) Attach a 4mm jump ring to center top of earring finding; attach a 4mm jump ring to bottom loop of ear wire. Attach both jump rings together.

4) Glue rhinestone to center of earring finding; let dry.

5) Repeat steps 1–4 for second earring. ●

Source: Gem adhesive from Duncan.

Fruit Punch

Designs by **Katie Hacker,** courtesy of Beadalon

Combine bubbly glass beads with stunning silver accents to create this one-of-a-kind jewelry set.

INSTRUCTIONS

Necklace

1) Cut three lengths of wire that measure 19, 20 and 21 inches. Hold lengths of wire together. Slide on a crimp bead ½ inch from wire ends; thread wire ends through one of the rings of the clasp and back through crimp bead. Gently squeeze crimp bead with crimp pliers and trim excess wire.

2) String the following beads on wires: three 6mm orange, single spacer, two 8mm green, single spacer, 6mm blue, single spacer, two 8mm green, single spacer, three 6mm orange, single spacer, two 8mm green, single spacer, 6mm red, single spacer, two 8mm green, single spacer and three 6mm orange.

3) Beginning at the short end, place wire strands through the 3 into 1 connector.

4) Separate strands and string the following on top wire strand: 4mm red, single spacer, three 8mm orange, single spacer, two 8mm green, single spacer, 10mm red, single spacer, two 8mm green, single spacer, three 8mm orange, single spacer, two 8mm green and a single spacer.

5) String on a 10mm blue bead and repeat beading sequence in step 4, only in reverse. Attach a piece of tape after the last bead to secure beads in place.

6) String the following on the center wire strand: 4mm red, single spacer, two 8mm green, single spacer, three 6mm orange, single spacer, two 8mm green, single spacer, 6mm red, single spacer, two 8mm green, single spacer, three 6mm orange, single spacer, two 8mm green, single spacer, 6mm blue, single spacer, two 8mm green and single spacer.

7) String on three 6mm orange beads and repeat beading sequence in step 6, only in reverse and alternating the 6mm red and 6mm blue beads. Attach a piece of tape after the last bead.

8) String the following on the bottom wire strand: 4mm red, single spacer, 6mm orange, single spacer, 10mm red, single spacer, two 8mm green, single spacer, three 8mm orange, single spacer, two 8mm green, single spacer, 10mm blue, single spacer, two 8mm green, single spacer, three 8mm orange, single spacer, two 8mm green and single spacer.

9) String on a 10mm red bead and repeat the beading sequence in step 8, only in reverse.

MATERIALS

- 6 (4mm) red round glass beads
- 6mm round glass beads: 4 blue, 4 red and 59 orange
- 48 (8mm) orange round glass beads
- 78 (8mm) green rondelle glass beads
- 10mm round glass beads: 7 blue, 9 red and 2 orange
- 88 (6mm) silver single rondelle spacer beads
- 14 (6mm) silver double rondelle spacer beads
- 2 (10mm) silver embossed disk beads
- .018-inch-diameter 19-strand nylon-coated flexible beading wire
- 3 continuous loops silver bracelet memory wire
- 2 (5mm) silver round memory wire end caps
- 2 (1.5mm) silver crimp beads
- 2 (3 into 1) silver connectors
- 2 (1-inch) silver head pins
- 2 (1-inch) silver eye pins
- Silver S-hook clasp with attached jump rings
- 2 silver French ear wires
- Round-nose pliers
- Chain-nose pliers
- Crimp pliers
- Heavy-duty wire cutters
- Bead adhesive
- Tape

FINISHED SIZES

Necklace
  18½ inches (including clasp)

Bracelet
  Can adjust to fit most wrists

Earrings
  2 inches long

10) Remove tape from each wire strand and beginning at the long end, thread them through the 3 into 1 connector. Join strands together and string on the beading sequence in step 2, only in reverse.

11) String on a crimp bead and other ring half of clasp; thread wire ends back through crimp bead and trim excess wire.

Bracelet

1) Glue an end cap on one end of memory wire. Let set for several hours before proceeding.

2) Slide on the following: three 8mm orange, single spacer, 10mm red, single spacer and three 8mm orange.

3) Slide on a double spacer, two 8mm green and a double spacer.

4) Slide on three 6mm orange, single spacer, 10mm blue, single spacer and three 6mm orange.

5) Beginning with step 3, alternate between steps 2 and 4, beading the sequence in step 3 in between each beading sequence. String on beads until bracelet is desired length. Trim memory wire ¼ inch beyond last bead. *Note: Memory wire is hard to cut and will damage regular wire nippers. Always use heavy-duty wire cutters or memory-wire shears to cut wire coils.*

6) Glue an end cap to wire end; let set for several hours. ***Note:*** *For added security, add a couple drops of glue to last few beads on each end of bracelet.*

Earrings

1) Slide a silver disk bead on an eye pin; use round-nose pliers to form a loop above bead and trim excess wire. Attach loop to ear wire and secure closed with chain-nose pliers.

2) Slide a single spacer and a 10mm orange bead on a head pin; form a loop above top bead and trim excess wire. Attach loop to bottom of silver disk bead.

3) Repeat steps 1 and 2 for second earring. ●

Source: Glass beads, memory wire and findings from Beadalon.

Beads & Bubbles

Design by **Lisa Galvin**

Light and airy, this multi-strand necklace resembles clear, refreshing water.

MATERIALS

Assorted small and medium
   aqua beads
Assorted aqua hammered
   flat beads
Small mother-of-pearl
   nugget beads
Clear seed beads
6 silver clamshell bead tips
Small silver lobster claw clasp
2 (3 into 1) silver
   jewelry findings
2 (5mm) silver jump rings
3 (79-inch) lengths silk beading
   cord with attached needle
Thread conditioner
Chain-nose pliers
Crimp pliers
Jewelry glue

FINISHED SIZE

Approximately 27 inches
   (including clasp)

INSTRUCTIONS

1) Apply a thin coat of thread conditioner to beading cord lengths; let dry. Set two cord lengths aside.

2) Slide a seed bead on cord end without needle; tie a knot to secure. Apply a dot of glue to knot; let dry. Beginning on the inside of clamshell bead tip; string needle end of cord through hole in bead tip, pulling gently until knotted seed bead is caught inside cup. Close and crimp the cup to secure.

3) String on a small aqua bead and a seed bead; bring needle up and back through small aqua bead. Gently move beads approximately 1 inch from bead tip end. Tie a knot at top of aqua bead to hold it in place. In same manner and using a variety of small aqua and mother-of-pearl nugget beads, continue to string beads, positioning them approximately ½ inch apart, until strand measures approximately 31 inches.

4) To end the strand, insert needle, beginning on the outside, through opening of a bead tip. Insert needle through a seed bead; thread needle back around and through seed bead again, locking it in place. Tie a knot. Trim thread end and crimp the bead tip. Attach end to center loop on 3-strand finding by closing bead tip around loop; repeat for other end, attaching it to center loop on other 3-strand finding.

5) Repeat step 2 for another length of cord. Randomly string on sections of seed beads and sections of aqua beads interspersed with mother-of-pearl nugget beads until strand measures approximately 30 inches. Repeat step 4 to end strand and to attach ends to top loops on 3-strand findings.

6) Repeat step 2 for remaining length of cord. Beginning ½ inch from bead tip, tie a knot. String on a seed bead, two small aqua beads, seed bead, mother-of-pearl nugget, seed bead, mother-of-pearl nugget, seed bead, mother-of-pearl nugget, seed bead, two small aqua beads and a seed bead. Tie a knot.

7) Tie another knot ¾ inch from last knot; string on a seed bead, four small aqua beads, medium aqua bead, small aqua bead, medium aqua bead, hammered flat bead, small aqua bead, two medium aqua beads, three small aqua beads and a seed bead. Tie a knot.

8) Tie another knot ¾ inch from last knot and repeat beading sequence in step 6. Tie a knot.

9) Tie another knot ¾ inch from last knot and string on the following: seed bead, five small aqua beads, three medium aqua beads, hammered flat bead, four medium aqua beads, three small aqua beads and a seed bead. Tie a knot.

10) Repeat step 8. CONTINUED ON PAGE 125

Beauty Washed Ashore

Design by **Katherine McBee**

The look of exotic shells and driftwood is easy to create with inexpensive beads.

INSTRUCTIONS

1) Cut a 22-inch length of beading wire; tape one end of wire to work surface. String on approximately 109 mother-of-pearl nugget beads. Tape end of wire and set aside.

2) Cut a 23-inch length of beading wire. Determine center of wire and string on leaf pendant. Twist wire around itself twice at top of pendant to secure pendant in place.

3) On one side of pendant, string three voluta shells and three mother-of-pearl nuggets.

4) String on a voluta shell, a wooden bead, a voluta shell and a mother-of-pearl nugget; repeat twice.

5) String on a voluta shell, a wooden bead, a voluta shell and three mother-of-pearl nuggets. Repeat three times.

6) String on a voluta shell, a wooden bead, three voluta shells, a mother-of-pearl nugget and two voluta shells. Tape end of wire to work surface.

7) Repeat steps 3–6 on other side of pendant.

8) To attach beaded strands together, place one end of the mother-of-pearl nugget strand together with one end of the carved wooden bead strand. Adjust strands to lie against each other; with strands together, string on four to five voluta shell beads. String on a crimp bead and one half of clasp; thread strand ends back through crimp bead and the voluta shell beads. Gently squeeze crimp bead with crimp pliers and trim wire. Repeat for other side of necklace, attaching remaining half of clasp.

9) Cut a 3-inch piece of beading cord and string on one mother-of-pearl nugget. Thread both cord ends through front hole on leaf pendant and double knot on back. ***Note:*** *Make knot large enough so it will not slip through pendant hole.* Apply a dot of jewelry glue to knot and trim cord. ●

Sources: Heart necklace starter kit from Cousin Corp. of America; pendant and beads from The Beadery; beading cord from Beadalon.

MATERIALS

- Heart necklace starter kit (includes toggle clasp, wire and crimp beads)
- Leaf shell pendant
- Small square voluta shell beads
- Mother-of-pearl nugget beads
- Carved wooden beads
- 1mm elastic beading cord
- Wire nippers
- Crimp pliers
- Masking tape
- Jewelry glue

FINISHED SIZE

Approximately 18 inches

Emerald Sea Bracelet

Design by **Katherine McBee**

Whether you live by the Emerald Sea or just dream of being there, this bracelet will remind you of the sun sparkling on the gentle waves.

Project note: When stringing beads onto each strand, secure remaining strands to a smooth surface with tape.

MATERIALS

Lime green seed beads

5 (16-inch) lengths of .015-
    inch-diameter green wire

Gold-tone toggle clasp

Wire nippers

Masking tape

FINISHED SIZE

7 inches

INSTRUCTIONS

1) Insert 2½ inches of all five lengths of wire through one end of toggle clasp; wrap ends around wire strands keeping wire as close as possible to the hole at the end of toggle clasp. Secure wire ends by threading them back under several wrapped wire strands. Trim excess wire.

2) String lime green seed beads on each wire strand until desired length is achieved.

3) Hold the outer two wires on each side together to form three pieces; braid wires together.

4) Insert wire ends through remaining half of clasp; secure in same manner as in step 1. Trim excess wire. ●

Sources: Crimp tool from The Beadery; seed beads from Sulyn Industries; green wire from Nicole Crafts; clasp from Blue Moon Beads.

Shades of Green

Design by **Lisa Galvin**

Mimicking the look and color of jade, these inexpensive beads create a look that will fool even your most fashion-forward friends.

MATERIALS

Silver 2-strand cable
    necklace kit
Assorted sizes green jade beads
Silver seed beads
2 (4mm) silver jump rings
Round-nose pliers
Chain-nose pliers

FINISHED SIZE

15¼ inches with a
    3-inch extender

INSTRUCTIONS

1) Bring cable ends together so that cable is folded in half. Onto what will be the inside strand, slide six silver seed beads. Slide two small jade beads and three silver seed beads onto cable; repeat this sequence four times. String three additional silver seed beads onto cable.

2) Slide the following beads onto other side of cable: two medium jade beads, one large jade bead, two medium jade beads and one small jade bead. Repeat this sequence five times leaving off the last small jade bead.

3) Secure wire by placing wire ends in eye crimp included in kit; use chain-nose pliers to squeeze closed. Open a 4mm jump ring with round-nose pliers; attach to extension chain on eye crimp. Close jump ring.

4) Attach remaining eye crimp to opposite end of necklace (the folded side); squeeze closed with chain-nose pliers. Use round-nose pliers and a 4mm jump ring to attach lobster claw clasp to eye crimp. ●

Source: Cable necklace kit from Hirschberg Schutz & Co.; seed beads and jade beads from The Beadery.

Seafoam & Sand

Designs by **Margot Potter**

Inspired by fashionable designs in a popular catalog, this set was created at a fraction of the cost! Use Swarovski crystal pearls and silver-plated chain for an affordable and fashionable look.

MATERIALS

7 (12mm) light green
    Swarovski crystal pearls
Small silver cable chain
7 (22-gauge) sterling silver
    eye pins
4 sterling silver jump rings
Small silver toggle clasp
2 sterling silver French
    ear wires
Round-nose pliers
Chain-nose pliers
Flush-cut wire cutters

FINISHED SIZES

Necklace
    17½ inches (including clasp)
Earrings
    3¼ inches long

INSTRUCTIONS

Necklace

1) Slide a pearl on an eye pin; use round-nose pliers to form a loop above pearl and trim excess wire. Repeat to make four additional pearl eye pins. Set eye pins aside.

2) Cut 18 (2¼-inch) lengths of cable chain. Separate lengths into six groups of three.

3) Open a jump ring and slide on one half of toggle clasp and one set of three chain lengths; use chain-nose pliers to close jump ring. Attach opposite ends of chain lengths to one loop on a pearl eye pin; close loop.

4) Attach another set of three lengths of chain to remaining loop on pearl eye pin. Continue attaching pearl eye pins and sets of chain lengths together in same manner. Use jump ring to attach remaining half of toggle clasp to ends of last set of chain lengths.

Earrings

1) Slide a pearl on an eye pin; form a loop above pearl and trim excess wire. Attach eye pin to ear wire. Secure loop closed with chain-nose pliers.

2) Cut three 1⅞-inch lengths of chain. Slide one end of each length of chain on a jump ring; attach jump ring to bottom loop on pearl eye pin.

3) Repeat steps 1 and 2 for second earring. ●

Source: Cable chain and toggle clasp from Beadalon.

Seaside Soiree

Designs by **Katie Hacker**

Pretty enough for an elegant dinner, yet simple enough for lunch with friends, this set will be summertime staple!

MATERIALS

65 (6mm) light gold round
   glass pearls
5 (10mm) dark gold square
   freshwater pearls
4 gold seed beads
4 (8mm) gold oval beads
18 inches .018-inch-diameter
   19-strand nylon-coated
   flexible gold beading wire
17 inches gold jewelry chain
   with open links
Gold toggle clasp
2 gold jump rings
2 gold crimp tubes
9 (1-inch) gold head pins
2 gold ear wires
Round-nose pliers
Chain-nose pliers
Crimp pliers
Wire nippers

FINISHED SIZES

Necklace
17 inches (including clasp)
Earrings
1¼ inches long

INSTRUCTIONS

Necklace

1) String a crimp tube ½ inch from one end of beading wire; thread wire end through one half of clasp and back through crimp tube. Gently squeeze crimp tube with crimp pliers. String on 28 glass pearls.

2) String on a gold oval bead; string on five square pearls, separating each one with a seed bead. String on a gold oval bead. String on 28 glass pearls.

3) String on a crimp tube and attach other half of clasp in same manner as in step 1. Trim excess wire.

4) Open a jump ring and slide on one end of jewelry chain; attach jump ring to one end of clasp. Close jump ring with chain-nose pliers. Attach remaining end of chain to other half of clasp in same manner.

5) Slide a glass pearl on a head pin; use round-nose pliers to form a loop above pearl. Trim excess wire. Repeat to make seven pearl head pins in total. Attach pearl head pins, evenly spaced, on center of chain.

Earrings

1) Slide a gold oval bead and a glass pearl on a head pin; form a loop above pearl and trim excess wire. Attach loop to ear wire. Secure loop closed with chain-nose pliers.

2) Repeat step 1 for second earring. ●

Sources: Square freshwater pearls from Thunderbird Supply Co.; glass pearls, beading wire and findings from Beadalon.

Beach Bag Charms

Designs by **Margot Potter**

Give your beach bag a new kick with these fabulously trendy charms.

OCEAN TALISMAN MATERIALS

Abalone green flat oval bead

Shell spine bead

Silver square toggle

2 silver jump rings

2 sterling silver ball-tipped head pins

8⅞ inches silver medium curb chain

Silver lobster claw clasp

Round-nose pliers

Chain-nose pliers

Flush-cut wire cutters

INSTRUCTIONS

Ocean Talisman

1) Cut a piece from curb chain that measures 3 links long; cut another piece that measures 6 links long and another piece that measures 7 links long.

2) Use chain-nose pliers to open a link on one end of the remaining long piece of curb chain and attach lobster claw clasp. Attach a jump ring to other end of curb chain.

3) Place the abalone bead on a head pin; use round-nose pliers to form a wrapped head pin loop above bead, attaching loop to one end of 3-link piece of curb chain before wrapping.

4) Place shell spine bead on a head pin; carefully bend head pin to form a hook shape so spine bead will hang down from head pin. Form a wrapped head pin loop above bead, attaching loop to one end of 6-link piece of curb chain before wrapping.

5) Open a link on one end of remaining 7-link piece of curb chain and use remaining jump ring to attach toggle; close link.

6) Attach each piece of chain to jump ring on 6-inch piece of chain.

Golden Turtle

1) Place each crystal pearl on a head pin; use round-nose pliers to form a loop above each crystal pearl. Trim excess wires.

2) Place cloisonné cylinder bead on remaining head pin; cut off the head part of the head pin and form a loop at each end.

3) Attach crystal pearls to turtle charm; connect turtle charm to one end of cloisonné cylinder bead head pin. Set aside.

4) Attach a jump ring to each end of chain; attach one half of toggle clasp to each jump ring. Attach assembled beaded head pin to one end of toggle clasp.

Coral, Shell & Crystal KJL-Inspired

1) Cut a piece from curb chain that measures 4 links long; cut another piece that measures 6 links long and another piece that measures 9 links long.

2) Open a jump ring and attach toggle end of clasp; attach jump ring to one end of remaining long piece of curb chain and close jump ring.

3) Open up last link on remaining end of long piece of curb chain and attach bar end of toggle clasp and another jump ring; close link.

4) Place mother-of-pearl pendant on ball-tipped head pin; carefully bend head pin to form a hook shape so pendant hangs down. Form a loop above pendant; attach loop to one end of 9-link piece of curb chain. Slide a coral branch bead on a head pin; form a loop above bead and attach it to loop above mother-of-pearl pendant. Trim excess wires.

5) Place a faceted pearl on a head pin; cut off head part of pin and form a loop at both ends. Trim excess wire. Place a teardrop bead on a head pin; form a loop above bead and attach it to bottom loop on pearl. Slide a coral branch bead on a head pin; form a loop above bead and attach it to bottom loop on pearl. Attach assembled piece to one end of 4-link piece of curb chain.

6) Repeat step 5 to make another beaded piece and attach it to one end of 6-link piece of curb chain. Attach all beaded pieces to jump ring next to bar end of toggle clasp. ●

Sources: Clasps and findings from Beadalon; abalone bead, shell spine bead, mother-of-pearl pendant, coral branch beads and ball-tipped head pins from Great Craft Works; square toggles from Blue Moon Beads.

GOLDEN TURTLE
MATERIALS

Cloisonné blue and gold cylinder bead

Cloisonné turtle charm

12mm copper and 8mm gold crystal pearls

2 gold jump rings

3 gold head pins

Large gold toggle clasp

6⅞ inches gold curb chain

Round-nose pliers

Chain-nose pliers

Flush-cut wire cutters

CORAL, SHELL
& CRYSTAL
KJL-INSPIRED
MATERIALS

Mother-of-pearl fan pendant

2 (6mm) faceted oval white pearls

2 (9 x 6mm) clear crystal teardrop beads

3 coral short branch beads

2 silver jump rings

Silver ball-tipped 20-gauge head pin

7 (24-gauge) sterling silver head pins

9⅛ inches silver medium curb chain

Silver toggle clasp

Round-nose pliers

Chain-nose pliers

Flush-cut wire cutters

Pink & Green Elegance

Design by **Katherine McBee**

Two-tone beads are even more eye-catching when paired with gold accents.

Project note: When stringing beads onto each strand, secure remaining strands to a smooth surface with tape.

INSTRUCTIONS

1) To make dangle charms, slide purple seed bead, pink/green diamond bead and another purple seed bead onto a decorative head pin; use round-nose pliers to form a loop above top bead. Trim excess wire. Repeat to make 12 dangle charms in total.

2) Hold both strands of thread together and fold in half to determine center. String three gold-tone ball beads through both threads and slide to center.

3) On one side of ball beads, separate strands and string a purple seed bead on each strand.

4) Bring strands together and thread a purple seed bead.

5) Separate strands and string a purple seed bead, dangle charm and a purple seed bead on each strand.

6) Repeat step 4.

7) Separate strands and string a purple seed bead, cylinder bead and a purple seed bead on each strand.

8) Repeat step 4.

9) Repeat step 5.

10) Repeat step 4.

11) Repeat step 5.

12) Hold strands together and string on a purple seed bead, gold cap spacers, round bead, gold cap spacer and a purple seed bead. *Note: String on gold cap spacers so they hold round bead in place.*

13) Separate strands and string a purple seed bead, gold cap spacer, round bead, gold cap spacer and a purple seed bead.

14) Repeat step 4.

15) Separate strands and string a purple seed bead, cylinder bead and a purple seed bead.

16) String a crimp bead onto one strand and insert thread end through one hole in one half of filigree clasp. Insert thread back through crimp bead and gently squeeze crimp bead with crimp tool. Repeat for other side of strand. Trim excess thread.

17) Repeat steps 3–16 for remaining side of bracelet, attaching other half of filigree clasp. ●

Sources: Clasp, head pins, ball beads and spacers from Blue Moon Beads; round, cylinder, oval and glass beads from Cousin Corp. of America.

MATERIALS

Purple seed beads

8 pink/green cylinder beads

12 pink/green diamond beads

6 pink/green round beads

3 gold-tone ball beads

12 gold-tone cap spacers

4 gold-tone crimp beads

2 (10-inch) lengths
monofilament thread

Gold double-strand filigree
box clasp

12 decorative gold-tone
head pins

Masking tape

Crimp pliers

Round-nose pliers

Wire nippers

FINISHED SIZE

6 inches

Summer Sorbet

Design by **Jennifer Mayer Fish**

A girl can never have too many bracelets and this brightly colored one will fit nicely in your collection.

Project note: Bracelet is made to wrap twice around wrist.

MATERIALS

Silver charms: star, dragonfly
    and double hearts
4 silver spacer bead frames
6mm rectangular beads in
    assorted colors
6mm white frosted
    rondelle beads
6mm blue rondelle beads
Pink wavy donut beads
Silver rondelle spacer beads
Silver crimp beads
3 (6mm) silver jump rings
Silver decorative toggle clasp
.015-inch-diameter 19-strand
    nylon-coated flexible
    beading wire
Chain-nose pliers
Crimp pliers
Wire nippers

FINISHED SIZE

15¼ inches (including clasp)

INSTRUCTIONS

1) Cut an 18-inch length of beading wire. Thread a crimp bead ½ inch from one end of wire; thread wire end through the bar end half of the toggle clasp and back through crimp bead. Gently squeeze crimp bead with crimp pliers and trim excess wire.

2) String on an assortment of beads for approximately 2 inches. String wire through one end of a bead frame. Before stringing wire through other side of bead frame, string on a white frosted or blue rondelle bead, a silver spacer and another white frosted or blue rondelle bead. Thread wire through other end of bead frame.

3) Repeat step 2 three additional times.

4) String on an assortment of beads for approximately 2 inches.

5) String on a crimp bead and other half of toggle clasp; thread wire end back through crimp bead and a few other beads. Gently squeeze crimp bead and trim excess wire.

6) Open a jump ring and slide on a silver charm; attach jump ring to round end of toggle clasp. Use chain-nose pliers to close jump ring. In same manner, attach remaining charms to round end of toggle clasp. ●

Sources: Charms from Magenta; spacer bead frames and rondelle beads from Westrim Crafts; beading wire from Beadalon; toggle clasp, wavy donut beads and rondelle spacer beads from Blue Moon Beads.

Amethyst Drops

Design by **Vicki Blizzard**

Accent this pretty beaded watchband with both silver and gold beads to have a fashion accessory that complements your other jewelry!

INSTRUCTIONS

1) Cut wire into two 12-inch strands. Thread one strand through one end of watch face and center.

2) On each end of wire, thread an amethyst bead, a silver heishe, a round mother-of-pearl bead, a silver heishe and an amethyst bead.

3) Bring both ends of wire together and thread through a gold heishe, an oval mother-of-pearl bead and a gold heishe.

4) Separate wires and repeat step 2.

5) Repeat step 3, adding an amethyst bead, a silver heishe, a round mother-of-pearl bead and a silver heishe after second gold heishe.

6) Thread both ends of wire through gold crimp tube, one end of toggle clasp and back through gold crimp tube. Crimp and fold crimp tube; trim wire ends.

7) Repeat steps 1–6 for second half of watchband, attaching remaining end of toggle clasp. ●

Sources: Beading wire from Beadalon.

MATERIALS

- 1 x 1¼-inch silver with gold accents watch face
- 18 (5mm) amethyst round beads
- 10 (5mm) white mother-of-pearl round beads
- 4 (6 x 8mm) white mother-of-pearl oval beads
- 20 (4mm) silver heishe beads
- 8 (4mm) gold heishe beads
- 2 gold crimp tubes
- 24 inches .015-inch-diameter 49-strand nylon-coated flexible beading wire
- Crimp pliers
- Wire nippers

FINISHED SIZE

8½ inches (including clasp)

Links & Rings

Design by **Jacki Jones**

Wire-wrapped beads swirl and shimmer around your wrist when combined with beaded jump rings.

MATERIALS

Wire-wrapped beads with two
    loops: 4 blue, 4 purple
18 blue purple-lined
    square beads
9 white mini glass pearls
9 (12mm) silver jump rings
Silver lobster-claw clasp
Round-nose pliers
Chain-nose pliers
Gem adhesive (optional)

FINISHED SIZE

7½ inches

INSTRUCTIONS

1) Open a jump ring; slide on clasp, square bead, blue wire-wrapped bead, square bead and a pearl. *Note: Openings on pearls are too small to allow pearl to move very far on jump ring.* Close jump ring. If needed, secure pearls on ends of jump rings with gem adhesive.

2) Open another jump ring; slide on opposite loop on blue wire-wrapped bead, square bead, purple wire-wrapped bead, square bead and a pearl. Close jump ring.

3) Continue repeating steps 1 and 2 to attach remaining jump rings and wire-wrapped beads, alternating colors of wire-wrapped beads. Bracelet should end with a beaded jump ring. ●

Sources: Wire-wrapped beads and pearls from Halcraft USA Inc.; square beads from Blue Moon Beads; clasp and jump rings from Westrim Crafts.

Snowballs Bangle

Design by **Vicki Blizzard**

Reminiscent of frosty blue raspberry and ice cream-flavored snowballs, this bracelet is cool and refreshing.

Project note: *Memory wire is hard to cut and will damage regular wire nippers. Always use heavy-duty wire cutters or memory-wire shears to cut wire coils.*

INSTRUCTIONS

1) Glue an end cap to one end of memory wire; let glue set for several hours before proceeding.

2) String on a cube bead, gold heishe bead, two saucer beads and a gold heishe bead. Repeat stringing sequence until beads are gone or until bracelet is desired length.

3) Trim memory wire ¼ inch beyond last bead. *Note: Leaving a small amount of excess wire between beads allows the beads to move on the bracelet and helps prevent the end cap from popping off from the pressure of tight beads.* Glue remaining end cap to end of wire; let glue set several hours. ●

Sources: Memory wire and end caps from Beadalon; GS Hypo Cement from Germanow-Simon Corp.

MATERIALS

- 20 (5mm) frosted clear glass cube beads
- 38 (8mm) light blue glass transparent and translucent fluted saucer beads
- 38 (4mm) gold heishe beads
- 2 coils of large bracelet memory wire
- 2 (3mm) round gold memory wire end caps
- Heavy-duty wire cutters
- Jewelry glue

FINISHED SIZE

Will fit most wrists

Sea Diva

Design by **Lisa Galvin**

Whatever the season, a pendant made of rainbow shell reflects nature at its finest.

MATERIALS

Oval Paua shell
    rainbow pendant
5 into 1 gold round chandelier
    necklace finding
4 (6mm) gold jump rings
18-gauge black wire
25 inches 1mm black round
    leather lace
Round-nose pliers
Chain-nose pliers
Wire nippers

FINISHED SIZE

24 inches

Project note: *This necklace is made to fit over the head. If length is not long enough, simply use a longer piece of leather lace.*

INSTRUCTIONS

1) Cut two ⅞-inch lengths of black wire; use round-nose pliers to form both pieces into "S" shapes. Attach shell pendant onto the bottom loop of one of the "S" wires, closing loop securely. Attach top loop of wire to bottom center loop on chandelier finding. Connect remaining "S" wire to top loop on chandelier finding.

2) Open a jump ring and slide it onto one of the remaining loops on chandelier finding; close jump ring. Repeat, attaching a jump ring to all remaining loops on finding.

3) Knot ends of leather lace together. Connect pendant to center of leather lace with loop on top "S" wire. Close loop. ●

Sources: Pendant and wire from The Beadery; leather lace from Tandy Leather Co.

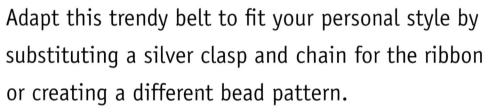

Bedazzling Sash Belt

Design by **Candie Cooper**

Adapt this trendy belt to fit your personal style by substituting a silver clasp and chain for the ribbon or creating a different bead pattern.

INSTRUCTIONS

1) String one crimp bead 3 inches from end of beading wire; string on a 2-inch section of E beads. Bring the wire end around to form a beaded loop; thread wire end through the crimp bead, leaving a 1-inch wire tail. Push crimp bead up so that beaded loop is snug; crimp the crimp bead with crimp pliers.

2) String on a small bead and another crimp bead. Crimp the crimp bead to secure the wire tail.

3) String approximately 32 inches of beads. String on a crimp bead, a small bead and another crimp bead. String a 2-inch section of E beads. Form a loop with the E beads by bringing the end of the wire down through the crimp bead, small bead and other crimp bead. Pull wire end carefully so there are no gaps in beaded strand. Crimp both crimp beads. Thread excess wire through beads.

4) Cut ribbon in half. On one end of one ribbon half, fold the top left corner down, meeting up with the right edge of the ribbon, forming a right triangle. Fold the top right point of the triangle down so that it lines up with the bottom left corner to make a peak; pin in place.

5) Thread needle and sew a few stitches to hold ribbon peak in place. Thread the ribbon peak through one of the beaded loops; fold peak over and pin in place. Sew the two layers together.

6) Repeat steps 4 and 5 for remaining ribbon half, attaching it to opposite beaded loop.

7) Trim ribbon ends at an angle. Apply seam sealant to ribbon ends to prevent fraying. ●

Source: Accu-Flex beading wire from Fire Mountain Gems & Beads.

MATERIALS

- Assorted beads in various shapes, sizes and colors
- Clear E beads
- 4 silver crimp beads
- 1¾ yard 1½-inch-wide black satin ribbon
- Black sewing thread
- 38 inches .014-inch-diameter 21-strand flexible beading wire
- Straight pins
- Sewing needle
- Crimp pliers
- Wire nippers
- Seam sealant

FINISHED SIZE

93 inches; beaded portion measures 35 inches

Faux Stone

Designs by **Linda Peterson**

The masculine look of turquoise is striking whether made from polymer clay or stone.

Project note: Use caution when using polymer clay blade. It is very sharp.

INSTRUCTIONS

Beads

1) Cool packages of clay by putting them into a refrigerator for ten minutes. Remove clay from refrigerator and cut up small amounts of turquoise, translucent and green clay.

2) For nugget bead, condition clay by mixing some of the cut-up pieces together and kneading clay with hands until it is warm and pliable. Do not knead it so much that the colors mix together and create a new color. Form a small amount of clay into a nugget shape. Use a needle tool to gently pierce a hole through the center of nugget. Set aside.

3) For disk beads, place several cut-up pieces of clay onto a disposable plate. Cover clay pieces with black paint; let dry.

4) Mix the pieces together in same manner as in step 2. Slice through center of clay to expose marbling effect. Flatten clay slightly to create an even sheet. Wrap sheet around bamboo skewer; smooth seam. Set aside.

5) Take a small amount of brown clay and flatten slightly, forming an even sheet. Wrap sheet around bamboo skewer; smooth seam.

6) Place nugget bead and clay-covered skewers on bead baking rack; bake in oven for approximately 30 minutes at 265 degrees, following manufacturer's instructions.

7) Let clay cool. Paint nugget bead black; let dry. Sand off some paint, allowing paint to remain in cracks of bead.

8) Remove bamboo skewers; sand clay lightly. Carefully slice clay into several uneven disk beads.

Necklace

1) Cut a 25 to 30-inch length of leather cord. Form a medium-sized loop on one end of cord and tie a knot around base of loop to secure.

2) Slide nugget bead or disk beads, along with any desired silver beads, onto cord. Position beads centered on cord. Tie a knot in cord on both sides of beads, securing them in place.

3) Tie a large double knot on remaining end of cord. If desired, knot cord 2 to 3 inches from end and slide on a silver bead before tying end knot. ●

Source: Clay, tools and baking rack from American Art Clay Co.

MATERIALS

- Polymer clay: turquoise, translucent, green, brown
- Desired silver beads
- Black leather cord
- Black acrylic paint
- 600-grit wet/dry sandpaper
- 2 bamboo skewers
- Disposable plate
- Bead baking rack
- Oven
- Paintbrush
- Needle tool
- Polymer clay blade *or* craft knife

FINISHED SIZE

Varies between 15¾ to 16¼ inches

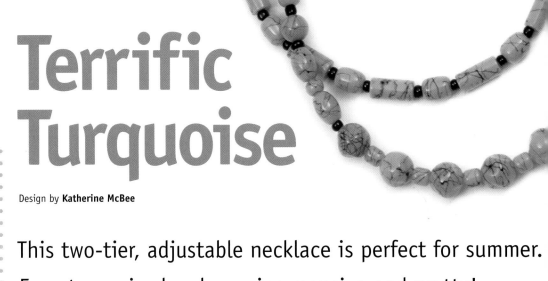

Terrific Turquoise

Design by **Katherine McBee**

This two-tier, adjustable necklace is perfect for summer. Faux turquoise beads are inexpensive and pretty!

MATERIALS

40 (6.5 x 4mm) black
round beads

8 (4mm) and 2 (10mm) faux
turquoise round beads

6 (10 x 8mm) faux turquoise
oval beads

13 (15 x 6mm) faux turquoise
long cylinder beads

14 (9 x 8mm) faux turquoise
medium cylinder beads

7 (6 x 5mm) faux turquoise
short cylinder beads

8 (11 x 10mm) faux
turquoise nuggets

Silver 2-tier cable necklace kit
(includes clasp, jump rings,
extension chain and
crimp ends)

Masking tape

Chain-nose pliers

Crimp pliers

Wire nippers

FINISHED SIZE

14½ inches plus a
3-inch extender

INSTRUCTIONS

1) Secure one end of bottom tier of cable wire with masking tape. String the following on wire: black round, two 4mm round, black round, long cylinder, black round, long cylinder, black round, oval, black round, medium cylinder, black round, 10mm round, black round, oval, 4mm round, oval and black round.

2) String on eight nuggets, separating each nugget with a short cylinder. Repeat beading sequence in step 1, only in reverse. Secure end with masking tape.

3) Secure one end of top tier of cable wire with masking tape. String the following on wire: black round, 4mm round, black round, medium cylinder, black round, medium cylinder and a black round.

4) Beginning and ending with a long cylinder, alternate stringing on nine long cylinders and eight medium cylinders, separating each with a black round.

5) Repeat beading sequence in step 3, only in reverse.

6) Push beads snugly against each other and carefully remove tape from one end; insert wire ends into crimp end. Gently squeeze crimp end to secure. Repeat for opposite wire ends. Trim excess wire if needed.

7) Open a jump ring and slide on clasp; attach jump ring to one end of necklace. Close jump ring with chain-nose pliers. Repeat for other end of necklace, attaching extension chain instead of clasp. ●

Sources: Beads from Cousin Corp. of America; cable necklace kit from Hirschberg Schutz & Co. Inc.

Dainty Delight

Design by **Lisa Galvin**

This easy-to-make bracelet is perfect for every day or for a night on the town.

Project note: When stringing on sliders, hold strands together.
When stringing on E beads, separate strands and string an E bead on each strand.

INSTRUCTIONS

1) Cut elastic beading cord in half, forming two 12-inch lengths. Tape both pieces together at one end.

2) String the following sequence on cords: two rectangle sliders, an E bead, a star slider, an E bead, two rectangle sliders, an E bead, two star sliders and an E bead. Repeat sequence two additional times.
Note: String on rectangle sliders so they curve toward the star slider in between the sets.

3) Remove tape and tie each strand together in a knot to secure; add a drop of glue to knots. Trim excess cord. ●

Sources: Metal sliders from Pure Allure Inc.; elastic beading cord from Beadalon.

MATERIALS

- Silver metal sliders: 9 small stars with green crystal insets and 12 rounded rectangles with clear crystal insets
- 24 silver-lined clear E beads
- 24 inches .032-inch-diameter clear elastic beading cord
- Jewelry glue
- Tape

FINISHED SIZES

2½ inches in diameter

Asian Artifact

Design by **Denise Gravano**

A "new jade" pendant gives this piece all the beauty and mystique of a buried treasure.

MATERIALS

New jade (serpentine) carved pendant

4 (4mm) gold glass beads

8 (4mm) alabaster round beads

4 (1½-inch) gold eye pins

Gold jump rings: 2 (6mm), 8 (3mm)

18 inches gunmetal medium cable chain with clasp

Round-nose pliers

Chain-nose pliers

Side cutters

FINISHED SIZE

22 inches (including clasp)

INSTRUCTIONS

1) Measure 5½ inches on each side of chain from the clasp down and cut. Cut remaining chain into four 1½-inch pieces.

2) Thread an alabaster bead, a gold bead and an alabaster bead on an eye pin. Use round-nose pliers to form a loop above top bead; trim excess wire. Repeat three additional times.

3) Open a 6mm jump ring and slide on pendant and an 1½-inch length of chain; close jump ring.

4) Attach a 3mm jump ring to end link on opposite end of 1½-inch length of chain, sliding on one loop of a beaded eye pin before closing jump ring.

5) In same manner, use 3mm jump rings to connect another 1½-inch length of chain, a beaded eye pin and one of the 5½-inch lengths of chain.

6) Repeat steps 4 and 5 for other side of necklace. ●

Sources: Pendant and alabaster beads from Revelations In Stone; gold beads from Rings & Things.

Silver Leaves

Design by **Margot Potter**

Dimensional metal leaves dangle from a chain of vintage glass beads to create a striking bracelet. This piece can hold its own with your chunkiest knits.

INSTRUCTIONS

1) Slide a barbell bead on an eye pin; use round-nose pliers to form a loop above bead. Trim excess wire. Repeat for remaining beads.

2) Use chain-nose pliers to open a jump ring; slide on the bar end of toggle clasp and another jump ring. Close jump ring. Open the second jump ring and slide on a leaf charm and one loop of an eye pin with an oval bead. Close jump ring.

3) In same manner, attach a jump ring to other end of eye pin. With jump ring open, slide on a leaf charm and one loop of an eye pin with a barbell bead on it. Close jump ring.

4) Continue attaching charms and eye pins together in this manner, alternating beads and attaching a charm between each one.

5) When there is one leaf charm left, open last jump ring and slide on the leaf charm, remaining loop of eye pin on end of bracelet and remaining half of clasp. Close jump ring securely. ●

Sources: Charms from Beads & Rocks; clasp from Blue Moon Beads.

MATERIALS

- 3 vintage German glass striated red barbell beads
- 3 vintage German glass textured black flat oval beads
- 7 silver dimensional leaf charms
- 8 (4mm) silver heavy-duty jump rings
- 6 silver eye pins
- Silver Bali square toggle clasp
- Round-nose pliers
- Chain-nose pliers
- Flush cutters

FINISHED SIZE

8 inches (including clasp)

Honey Drops

Designs by **Vicki Blizzard**

Round honey stones and yellow calcite nuggets resemble chunks of solidified honey mixed with cream. The rich neutral color of these pieces looks great with any color outfit—especially plum!

MATERIALS

12 (12mm x 18mm) yellow
    calcite nugget beads
40 (8mm) honey stone
    round beads
20 (4mm x 6mm) gold
    corrugated oval beads
76 (3mm) gold vermeil Bali
    daisy spacers
2 (9mm) gold lobster
    claw clasps
4 (5mm) gold jump rings
2 (2-inch) gold head pins
2 gold French ear wires
8 gold crimp beads
33 inches .015-inch-diameter
    49-strand nylon-coated
    flexible beading wire
Chain-nose pliers
Round-nose pliers
Wire nippers

FINISHED SIZES

Necklace
    21½ inches
Bracelet
    8 inches
Earrings
    1¾ inches long

INSTRUCTIONS

Necklace

1) Open a jump ring and place on lobster claw clasp. Close jump ring securely.

2) Cut a 24-inch length of beading wire. String two crimp beads ½ inch from end of beading wire; place wire end through jump ring attached to clasp and thread back through crimp beads. Use chain-nose pliers to flatten crimp bead furthest away from clasp.

3) String a daisy spacer, a round bead, a daisy spacer, a gold oval bead, a daisy spacer, a round bead, a daisy spacer and a nugget. Repeat stringing sequence 10 more times. String a daisy spacer, a round bead, a daisy spacer, a gold oval bead, a daisy spacer, a round bead and a gold daisy spacer.

4) String two crimp beads and jump ring. Thread end of wire back through crimp beads and several other beads. Use chain-nose pliers to flatten crimp bead furthest away from ring. Trim excess wire.

Bracelet

1) Follow steps 1 and 2 of necklace, cutting a 12-inch length of beading wire.

2) String a daisy spacer, a round bead, a daisy spacer, a gold oval bead, a daisy spacer and a round bead. Repeat stringing sequence two more times. String a daisy spacer, a nugget bead and a daisy spacer. Repeat beginning stringing sequence in reverse.

3) Repeat step 4 of necklace.

Earrings

1) On a gold head pin, thread a daisy spacer, a round bead, a daisy spacer, a gold oval bead, a daisy spacer, a round bead and a daisy spacer.

2) Form a wrapped loop, inserting ear wire through loop before wrapping. Trim excess wire.

3) Repeat steps 1 and 2 for remaining earring. ●

Source: Beading wire and clasps from Beadalon.

Back to Nature

Designs by **Katherine McBee**

Many of these fun beads were recycled from vintage pieces found at garage and estate sales. Keep your eyes open for treasures like these or substitute your own finds to create a unique set that expresses your personal style.

Project note: When stringing beads onto each strand, secure remaining strands to a smooth surface with tape.

INSTRUCTIONS

Necklace

1) Slide a small bead, elephant bead and a small bead onto head pin; use round-nose pliers to form a loop above top bead.

2) Hold both strands of 26-inch lengths of thread and fold in half to determine center. Thread elephant head pin onto center of threads.

3) With both strands together, string the following sequence on one side: small light-colored bead, dark-colored bead, carved bone bead, dark-colored bead, carved rectangle, small carved bone bead, light-colored bead, small carved bone bead, carved rectangle, small carved bone bead, small light-colored bead and small carved bone bead.

4) Separate strands and string 12 flat discs onto each strand.

5) Hold strands together and string a small carved bone bead, small bead, small carved bone bead and four medium beads.

6) Separate strands and string 27 flat discs onto each strand.

7) Keep strands separate and string a copper crimp bead onto each one. Insert one thread end through one hole in one half of toggle clasp; run thread back through crimp bead and gently squeeze crimp bead. Repeat for other strand.

8) Repeat steps 3–7 for other half of necklace, attaching remaining half of toggle clasp at end.

Bracelet

1) Alternating between large and small beads, string desired carved bone beads onto 16-inch length of clear elastic thread.

2) Tie a double knot at end and secure with jeweler's cement. ●

Source: Copper clasp and crimp beads from Blue Moon Beads.

MATERIALS

- Carved bone elephant bead
- Assorted shapes and sizes light- and dark-colored beads
- Assorted carved bone beads
- Small natural-color discs
- Copper crimp beads
- Copper toggle clasp with two holes
- Silver head pin
- 2 (26-inch) lengths mono-filament thread
- 1 (16-inch) length 0.5mm clear elastic thread
- Crimp pliers
- Round-nose pliers
- Masking tape
- Jeweler's cement
- Wire nippers

FINISHED SIZES

Necklace
  18½ inches
Bracelet
  Will accommodate small and large wrists

For a Cure

Design by **Katherine McBee**

A wrist full of pink beads with a tiny ribbon charm is a beautiful way to show your support for breast cancer awareness.

MATERIALS

2 (14-inch) lengths
  tiger tail thread
Silver-tone heart toggle clasp
Breast cancer awareness
  ribbon charm
Pink and white chip beads
Pink cat's eye beads
White cat's eye beads
Small pink Swarovski
  crystal beads
Clear Swarovski crystal beads
Silver sequin beads
Silver decorative head pins
Silver head pins
2 silver Bali spacer beads
4 silver Bali beads
4 silver pink crystal slides
Silver crimp beads
Silver jump ring
Masking tape
Round-nose pliers
Crimp tool
Wire nippers

FINISHED SIZE

7 inches

Project note: *When stringing beads onto each strand, secure remaining strands to a smooth surface with tape.*

INSTRUCTIONS

1) To create charms for the center of the bracelet, thread a pink crystal bead onto a plain head pin. Use round-nose pliers to form a loop above bead; trim excess wire. Repeat to make an additional single pink crystal charm. Attach both charms to another plain head pin to create a double charm. Repeat to make a total of 22 double charms.

2) For single charms, thread a clear crystal, silver sequin, white cat's eye or pink cat's eye bead onto a decorative or plain head pin. Form a loop above bead in same manner as in step 1. Repeat to make 22 single charms.

3) Holding both strands of tiger tail together, thread a crimp bead onto threads approximately ½ inch from end; thread tail ends through one half of toggle clasp and back through crimp bead. Gently squeeze crimp bead with crimp tool.

4) String on one Bali spacer and two Bali beads.

5) Separate strands and string five chips and a white cat's eye bead onto each strand.

6) String on a pink slide; string a pink cat's eye bead onto each strand. Repeat once.

7) Hold strands together and begin to attach single and double charms randomly. If desired, string pink chips in between charms.

8) Separate strands and string a pink cat's eye bead onto each strand; string on a pink slide. Repeat once.

9) Repeat step 5 in reverse.

10) Hold strands together and repeat step 4 in reverse.

11) String on a crimp bead; thread ends through remaining half of clasp and back through crimp bead. Gently squeeze crimp bead.

12) Attach ribbon charm to a jump ring and attach at one end of bracelet. ●

Sources: Heart clasp and decorative pin head pins from Blue Moon Beads; metal sliders from Pure Allure Inc.; cat's eye beads and Bali silver spacers from Imagine it.

Eye of the Tiger

Design by **Jacki Jones**

A metal charm adds just the right amount of "oomph" to this simply strung bracelet.

MATERIALS

Tiger's eye beads: 7 (6mm),
   3 (8mm), 3 (8mm x 12mm)

Bali beads: 4 large round,
   2 small round, 2 small
   cylinders, 2 large cylinders

Silver shoe charm

Silver jump ring

2 silver crimp beads

Silver toggle clasp

12 inches .015-inch-diameter
   19-strand nylon-coated
   flexible beading wire

Chain-nose pliers

Crimp pliers

Wire nippers

FINISHED SIZE

7½ inches (including clasp)

INSTRUCTIONS

1) String a crimp bead ½ inch from end of beading wire; place wire end through one half of clasp and back through crimp bead. Crimp the crimp bead.

2) String the following sequence on beading wire: small cylinder bead, 6mm tiger's eye, small round bead, 6mm tiger's eye, large cylinder bead, 8mm tiger's eye and a 6mm tiger's eye. String a large round bead, 8mm x 12mm tiger's eye and large round bead.

3) String on a 6mm tiger's eye, 8mm x 12mm tiger's eye and an 8mm tiger's eye. Repeat beading sequence in step 2, only in reverse.

4) String on a crimp bead and remaining half of clasp; place wire end back through crimp bead and several other beads. Crimp the crimp bead. Trim excess wire.

5) Open jump ring and slide on charm; attach jump ring to round clasp end of bracelet. Close jump ring. ●

Sources: Charm from Blue Moon Beads; beading wire from Beadalon.

Moroccan Magic

Design by **Margot Potter**

Unique silver findings combine with beads in Mediterranean-inspired colors for earrings that flatter everyone.

INSTRUCTIONS

1) Slide an olive jade square bead onto an eye pin; use round-nose pliers to create a loop above bead. Trim excess wire with flush cutters.

2) Open top loop on eye pin and attach to ear wire; secure loop with chain-nose pliers. Open bottom loop on eye pin and attach rectangle earring finding in same manner.

3) Slide a turquoise rondelle onto an eye pin; form a loop above rondelle in same manner as step 1. Repeat three more times.

4) Slide a dark pink rondelle onto an eye pin; form a loop in same manner as step 1.

5) Thread a leaf charm onto a jump ring; repeat two more times. Use round-nose pliers to join each leaf charm to the turquoise rondelle eye pins. Attach leaf dangles to the outside holes on earring finding, leaving one for center dangle.

6) For center dangle, attach dark pink rondelle to turquoise eye pin with leaf. Attach remaining turquoise eye pin to top of dark pink eye pin; attach dangle to center hole in earring finding.

7) Repeat steps 1–6 for second earring. ●

Sources: Metal leaf charms from Blue Moon Beads; 3 into 1 rectangle earring findings from Beadalon.

MATERIALS

- 2 (10mm) olive jade square beads
- 8 (4 x 6mm) turquoise faceted fire polished Czech glass rondelles
- 2 (4 x 6mm) dark pink striated A/B Czech glass rondelles
- 6 small silver leaf charms
- 6 (4mm) sterling silver jump rings
- 12 sterling silver 24-gauge eye pins
- 2 silver rectangle earring findings with 3 holes
- 2 sterling silver French ear wires
- Round-nose pliers
- Chain-nose pliers
- Flush cutters

FINISHED SIZE

3 inches long

Metallic Treasures

Designs by **Katherine McBee**

Copper is a hot color this season. Combine it with art glass beads in sizzling green and blue and you've got an unforgettable jewelry set for work or a night on the town!

MATERIALS

12 metallic round beads
10 metallic flat square beads
14 copper cylinder spiral beads
2 copper small round beads
10 copper large round beads
10 copper disc spacers
10 copper round spiral beads
Copper crimp beads
2 decorative copper head pins
2 copper flower toggle clasps
Copper earring findings
Tiger tail thread
Wire nippers
Round-nose pliers
Crimp pliers

FINISHED SIZES

Necklace
 17½ inches
Bracelet
 7½ inches
Earrings
 1 inch long

INSTRUCTIONS

Necklace

1) Cut a 22-inch piece of tiger tail. String one crimp bead onto thread approximately ½ inch from end; thread tail end through a hole in one half of toggle clasp and back through crimp bead. Gently squeeze crimp bead with crimp tool.

2) String one cylinder spiral bead, one copper small round bead and another cylinder spiral bead onto thread.

3) String one large round copper bead and a disc spacer onto thread. Repeat four additional times.

4) String one round metallic bead and a cylinder spiral bead. Repeat three additional times. String one additional round metallic bead.

5) String a copper round spiral bead and a square metallic bead. Repeat three additional times. String on an additional copper spiral bead.

6) Repeat step 4.

7) Repeat step 3 in reverse.

8) Repeat step 2.

9) String on a crimp bead and attach remaining half of toggle clasp in same manner as in step 1.

Bracelet

1) Cut a 13-inch piece of tiger tail. String on a crimp bead and attach one half of toggle clasp in same manner as in step 1 for necklace.

2) String on a cylinder spiral bead and a square metallic bead.

3) String on a copper round spiral bead and a square metallic bead. Repeat four additional times. String on a cylinder spiral bead.

4) String on a crimp bead and attach remaining half of clasp in same manner as in step 1.

CONTINUED ON PAGE 125

Smoke & Silver Bracelet

Design by **Vicki Blizzard**

Smoky lead-glass coupled with handcrafted Bali rings and beads create a unique bracelet that adds sparkle to a business suit or an evening dress.

Project notes: Nickel jump rings are stronger than sterling silver and should be used in this project to create a stronger bracelet. Use a jump ring tool for easier jump ring opening and closing.

MATERIALS

25 black diamond Swarovski crystals in assorted shapes and sizes

20–25 Bali beads in assorted shapes and sizes

17 (9mm) Bali twisted rings

17 (6mm) nickel jump rings

13mm sterling silver lobster claw clasp

25 Bali dot head pins

Chain-nose pliers

Round-nose pliers

Wire nippers

Jump ring tool (optional)

FINISHED SIZE

8 inches

INSTRUCTIONS

Bracelet

1) Open a jump ring and place two Bali twisted rings on jump ring; close jump ring. Continue adding and alternating jump rings and Bali twisted rings until bracelet is desired length. Model bracelet uses 17 Bali twisted rings.

2) Add last jump ring and attach lobster claw clasp before closing ring. To close bracelet, attach lobster claw to first Bali twisted ring.

Charms

1) For half of the charms, thread a Bali bead and a Swarovski crystal bead onto a dot head pin. Form a wrapped head pin loop above beads, attaching to a Bali twisted ring on bracelet before wrapping. Trim excess wire from head pin. **Note:** *Some links of bracelet will have one charm, some two, and a few will have three. Leave two Bali twisted rings closest to clasp free of charms for ease in closing clasp.*

2) For remaining half of the charms, thread a Swarovski crystal bead and a Bali bead onto a dot head pin and attach to bracelet in same manner as in step 1.

3) For any remaining crystal beads, thread a bead onto a dot head pin and attach to bracelet in same manner as in step 1. ●

Beachside Barbecue

Designs by **Katie Hacker**

MATERIALS

1¾-inch round brown
  shell pendant
2 (6mm) turquoise round beads
4 (8mm) turquoise
  trillion beads
24 (10mm) carnelian chips
2 (8mm) gold barrel beads
2 (8mm) gold oval beads
6 inches .018-inch-diameter
  19-strand nylon-coated
  flexible gold beading wire
13 inches brown suede lace
2 gold crimp tubes
3 gold jump rings
4 gold c-crimp cord ends
Gold S-hook clasp
Gold extension chain
2 gold ear wires
2 gold eye pins
Round-nose pliers
Chain-nose pliers
Crimp pliers
Wire nippers

FINISHED SIZES

Necklace
18¼ inches with a
  2-inch extender
Earrings
1¾ inches long

Remember summers past with a necklace created in the smoky shades of a fun-filled cookout at the beach.

INSTRUCTIONS

Necklace

1) Cut suede lace in half; use chain-nose pliers to secure a c-crimp cord end to each end of both pieces.

2) String a crimp tube ½ inch from one end of wire; thread wire end through one c-crimp cord end and back through crimp tube. Gently squeeze crimp tube with crimp pliers. String the following on wire: gold oval bead, turquoise trillion, nine carnelian chips and turquoise round.

3) Open a jump ring and slide on shell pendant; attach jump ring to wire and close jump ring with chain-nose pliers. Repeat beading sequence in step 2, only in reverse. String on a crimp tube and thread wire end through a c-crimp cord end on other piece of suede lace; place wire end back through crimp tube and crimp. Trim excess wire.

4) Open a jump ring and slide on S-hook clasp; attach jump ring to one end of necklace. Close jump ring. Repeat to attach extension chain to other end of necklace.

Earrings

1) Slide a gold barrel bead, three carnelian chips and a turquoise trillion on an eye pin; use round-nose pliers to form a loop above top bead and attach loop to ear wire. Close loop with chain-nose pliers; trim excess wire.

2) Repeat step 1 for second earring. ●

Sources: Beading wire, faux suede lace and findings from Beadalon; turquoise beads and carnelian chips from Thunderbird Supply Co.; shell pendant from Pure Allure Inc.

Copper Canyon

Design by **Margot Potter**

Inexpensive gemstones combined with copper beads and charms create this designer-looking piece for a fraction of the price. The mossy green shades create a timeless upscale look.

Project notes: *If desired, lay out beads and pearls in a multichannel bead board before stringing to ensure that the inner strand will nestle inside outer strand.*

MATERIALS

Approximately 41 (5mm x 6mm)
    khaki green rice
    freshwater pearls
Approximately 34 (4mm x 6mm)
    bronze rice freshwater pearls
1 (15mm x 20mm) pietersite
    rectangle bead
18 (8mm x 12mm) African
    green jasper rectangle beads
28 (4mm x 10mm) grossular
    garnet rondelle beads
9 copper flat grape with
    leaf charms
4 gold-plated crimp tubes
12 (2-inch-long) copper
    head pins
1 (2-inch-long) copper eye pin
Copper floral toggle clasp
2 (18-inch) lengths .013-inch-
    diameter 49-strand nylon-
    coated flexible beading wire
Multichannel bead board
    (optional)
Electric bead reamer
Round-nose pliers
Chain-nose pliers
Crimp pliers
Flush cutters

FINISHED SIZE

15¼ inches (including clasp)

INSTRUCTIONS

1) Use the bead reamer to widen the holes in 12 khaki rice pearls so they will accommodate the copper head pins.

2) Slide each reamed khaki rice pearl onto a separate head pin; using round-nose pliers, form wrapped head pin loops above each pearl. Trim excess wires. Do not throw away trimmed pieces of copper head pins.

3) Slide pietersite rectangle onto an eye pin; form a wrapped loop above rectangle. Trim excess wire.

4) Using scrap pieces from trimmed head pins and round-nose pliers, form seven handmade jump rings, setting three aside for use later. Open one jump ring and slide it onto bottom loop of pietersite eye pin; slide another handmade jump ring and a khaki rice head pin on first jump ring before closing ring. Open second ring and slide on a khaki rice head pin; close ring. Attach two additional handmade jump rings in same manner. Open last jump ring and slide on a copper charm; close jump ring.

5) Open one of the remaining three handmade jump rings and slide on bar end of clasp and another jump ring; close jump ring. In same manner, attach last jump ring to second jump ring.

6) String a crimp tube ½ inch from wire end on an 18-inch length of beading wire; place wire end through one half of clasp and back through crimp tube. Crimp the crimp tube.

7) Beginning and ending with a khaki rice pearl, string 29 khaki rice pearls and 28 rondelles, alternating between the two. This strand should measure approximately 14 inches. String on a crimp tube and place wire end through remaining half of clasp and back through crimp tube. Crimp the crimp tube. Trim excess wire.

CONTINUED ON PAGE 125

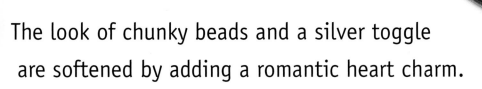

Bold Is Beautiful

Design by **Margot Potter**

The look of chunky beads and a silver toggle are softened by adding a romantic heart charm.

INSTRUCTIONS

1) Slide a crimp tube ½ inch from one end of beading wire; thread wire end through round half of toggle clasp and back through crimp tube. Gently squeeze and fold crimp tube in half with crimp tool.

2) Thread beads onto wire in the following sequence: heart charm, 2 brown rhodochrosite rectangles, a carnelian nugget, a bead cap, a carnelian nugget, a bead cap, a carnelian nugget and a flat silver-plated bead.

3) Slide on a crimp tube and a jump ring; thread wire end back through crimp tube and flat silver-plated bead. Gently squeeze and fold crimp tube in half.

4) Open jump ring and attach one end of each length of chain to jump ring; close jump ring. Open remaining ends of chain and attach each to remaining half of clasp. ***Note:*** *If chain is soldered, use jump rings to attach chains to toggle clasp.* ●

Sources: Carnelian nuggets from Thunderbird Supply Co.; rhodochrosite beads from Bead Warehouse; flat silver-plated bead, bead caps, heart charm and toggle clasp from Blue Moon Beads; crimp tubes, beading wire and chain from Beadalon.

MATERIALS

- 2 (20 x 15mm) brown rhodochrosite flat rectangles
- 3 carnelian nuggets
- 1 round flat silver-plated bead
- 2 swirl silver-plated bead caps
- Antiqued silver-plated heart charm
- 2 (1.3mm) silver crimp tubes
- Small silver-plated jump ring
- Large silver-plated toggle clasp
- 2 (11-inch) lengths elongated cable chain
- 5½ inches .018-inch-diameter 19-strand nylon-coated flexible beading wire
- Round-nose pliers
- Chain-nose pliers
- Flush cutters
- Crimp pliers

FINISHED SIZE

16½ inches

Regal Red

Design by **Margot Potter**

The texture, color and shine of this striking piece will turn you into a 21st century jazz babe!

INSTRUCTIONS

1) Slide a Nepalese bead on an eye pin; use round-nose pliers to form a loop above bead. Trim excess wire. Repeat for each Nepalese bead.

2) Open a loop on one end of an eye pin with a diamond-shaped Nepalese bead on it; slide loop onto round end of clasp. Close loop.

3) Open a 4mm jump ring and slide it on other end of eye pin attached to clasp. Slide an eye pin with a Nepalese round bead on jump ring; close jump ring. Continue to use 4mm jump rings to attach 11 additional beaded eye pins, alternating between diamond and round beads. This will form a beaded eye pin chain.

4) Repeat steps 2 and 3 to make another beaded eye pin chain, attaching first eye pin to remaining half of clasp with an 8mm jump ring. Each chain should end with a diamond-shaped beaded eye pin.

5) Open remaining 8mm jump ring and slide on ends of both chains and pendant; close jump ring.

6) Slide a bicone bead onto a head pin; use round-nose pliers to form a wrapped head pin loop above bead, attaching loop to one of the small jump rings between the beaded eye pins before wrapping. Trim excess wire.

7) Repeat step 6 for all of the bicone beads, attaching three beaded head pins to each small jump ring. Attach nine beaded head pins to the large jump ring in the center of the necklace. Go back through necklace, securing all loops and jump rings closed with chain-nose pliers. ●

Sources: Nepalese beads from A World of Good; clasp from Hirschberg Schutz & Co. Inc.; head pins from Beadalon; blown-glass pendant from Blue Moon Beads.

MATERIALS

- Blown-glass poppy pendant
- Two-tone Nepalese sterling silver beads: 14 diamond-shaped, 12 round
- 81 (4mm) hyacinth satin-finish Swarovski bicone crystal beads
- 81 silver-plated head pins
- 26 silver-plated eye pins
- Silver-plated jump rings: 24 (4mm), 2 (8mm)
- Silver-plated toggle clasp
- Round-nose pliers
- Chain-nose pliers
- Flush cutters

FINISHED SIZE

- 26½ inches (including clasp)

Leather & Unakite

design by **Lorine Mason**

The rich marbled look of unakite beads is distinctly masculine when intertwined with knotted black and brown leather cording.

Project note: String all beads on center black cord.

INSTRUCTIONS

1) Cut all cords into 1-yard lengths. Lay cords on work surface next to each other, alternating colors, starting and ending with black. Tie together with an overhand knot. Tape knot to work surface.

2) Slide a bead onto the center black cord. Tie a square knot. Make a square knot by crossing the right set of cords over the two base cords and under the two left cords, leaving a loop to the right (Fig. 1). *Note: Figures do not show both cords in each set to allow readability.* Cross the left cords under the two base cords and up through the loop (Fig. 2). Pull both outside cords to tighten. Cross the left set of cords (which are now on the right side) under the two base cords and over the right cords (now on the left side), leaving a loop to the right (Fig. 3). Cross the right set of cords over the base cords and through the loop (Fig. 4). Pull both outside cords to tighten the knot.

3) Leaving approximately ½-inch space, tie another square knot. Leave another ½-inch space and tie a square knot. String on a bead. Tie two square knots. Leave a ½-inch space; tie a square knot and leave a ½-inch space.

4) Tie a square knot; string on a bead and tie two square knots. String on a bead. Tie two square knots; string on a bead and tie a square knot.

5) Leave a ½-inch space; tie a square knot and leave another ½-inch space.

6) Repeat steps 2–4, only in reverse.

7) Trim ends of cords 1½ inches past last bead. Dip cord ends into glue. Slide leather cords into silver cord end; let dry.

8) Untie overhand knot on opposite end and repeat step 7.

9) Use a piece of trimmed cord and wrap it around the leather cords near one cord end, applying glue to secure. Trim excess cord. Repeat for remaining end.

10) Use needle-nose pliers to open end section on one silver cord end; slide on clasp. Close cord end securely. ●

Sources: Beads from Expo International Inc.; leather cord from Tandy Leather Co.; cord ends and clasp from Beadalon; super glue from The Adhesive Products Inc.

MATERIALS

- 10 (6mm) round unakite beads
- 2 (3.5mm) silver cord ends
- Silver lobster claw clasp
- 3 yards 1mm black leather cord
- 2 yards 1mm brown leather cord
- Needle-nose pliers
- Tape
- Water-based super glue

FINISHED SIZE

17 inches (including clasp)

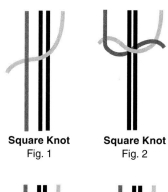

Square Knot
Fig. 1

Square Knot
Fig. 2

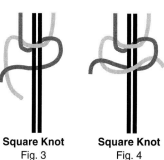

Square Knot
Fig. 3

Square Knot
Fig. 4

Frozen Colors

Design by **Vicki Blizzard**

The icy pastel colors of these dichroic glass beads will look spectacular against a little black dress! Glass artist Paula Radke has found a way to create these beads in mass quantities, making them affordable as well as beautiful.

MATERIALS

Dichroic glass beads:

  6 (7mm) cased green on clear cubes

  6 (7mm) cased pink on clear cubes

  6 (6 x 20mm) cased green on clear tubes

  6 (6 x 20mm) cased pink on clear tubes

  6 (7mm) cased green on clear rounds

  6 (7mm) cased pink on clear rounds

  2 (13mm) cased green on clear rounds

  1 (13mm) cased pink on clear round

  2 (10 x 19mm) green clear with pink clear stripe twisted

34 (4mm) sterling silver heishe spacer beads

Sterling silver "S" clasp with split rings

2 (2mm) silver crimp tubes

30 inches .030-inch-diameter 49-strand nylon-coated flexible beading wire

Crimp pliers

Wire nippers

FINISHED SIZE

20 inches

Project note: Place a silver heishe spacer in between each bead, except for between the two 7mm round beads. This is not specified in step 2 in order to keep the instructions simple.

INSTRUCTIONS

1) String a crimp tube ½ inch from end of beading wire; place wire end through one split ring end of clasp and back through crimp tube. Use crimp pliers to crimp and fold tube.

2) String beads in the following sequence: green cube, pink tube, green cube, pink tube, green cube, pink tube, green 7mm round, pink 7mm round, green tube, pink cube, green tube, pink cube, green tube, pink cube, 2-color twisted, green 7mm round, pink 7mm round, green 13mm round, pink 7mm round and green 7mm round.

3) String on pink 13mm round, which will be the center bead.

4) Repeat step 2 in reverse.

5) Repeat step 1, stringing remaining split ring end of clasp. ●

Sources: Dichroic beads from Paula Radke; crimp tubes and beading wire from Beadalon.

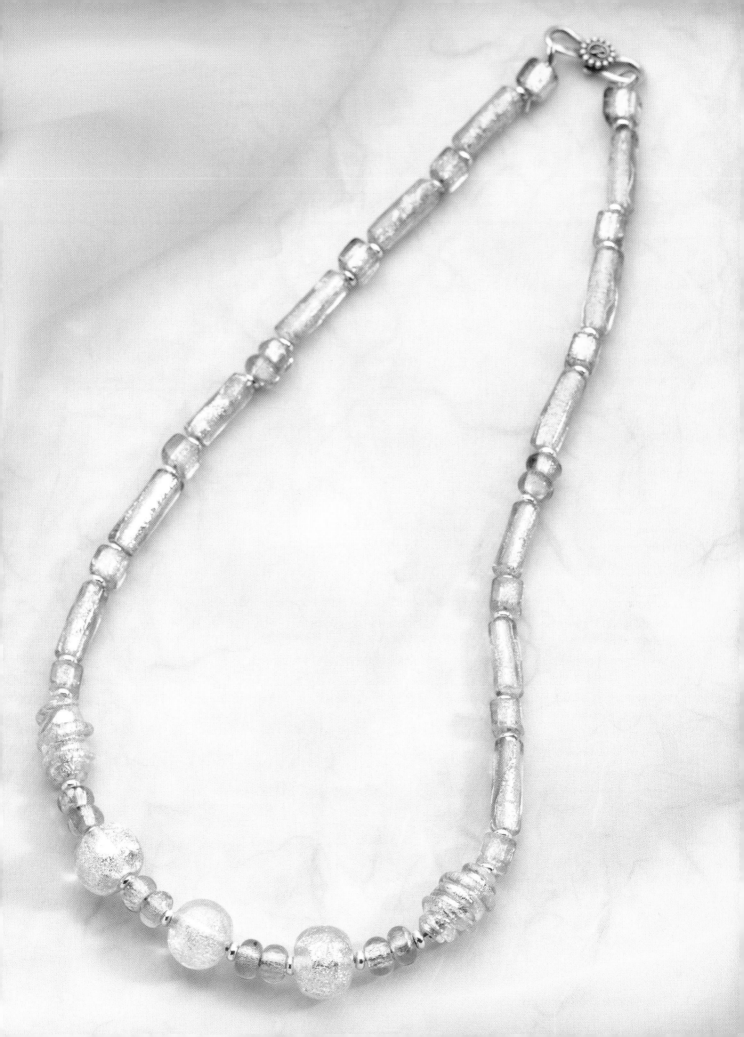

Night Sky

Design by **Nancy Hoerner**

This sophisticated necklace features tiny stars and shimmery beaded charms that reflect light with every movement. It's a fun, eclectic look and a great way to practice making wire loops.

INSTRUCTIONS

1) Slide approximately 20 clear seed beads on an eye pin; use round-nose pliers to form a loop above top bead and trim excess wire. Open one end of eye pin and attach a small star charm; use chain-nose pliers to secure eye-pin loop closed. Repeat to make 16 seed bead eye pins.

2) Slide approximately eight bugle beads on an eye pin; form a loop above top bead and trim excess wire. Open one end of eye pin and attach a medium star charm; close eye-pin loop. Repeat to make eight bugle bead eye pins.

3) Slide a silver spacer, a large round clear bead and a silver spacer on an eye pin; form a loop above top bead and trim excess wire. Find the center on the jewelry chain and attach beaded eye pin.

4) Lay chain out on work surface and attach all of the remaining beaded eye pins at equal intervals on each side of center beaded eye pin.

5) Slide a small round silver bead, a tube bead and a small round silver bead on a head pin; form a loop above top bead and trim excess wire. Repeat to make eight beaded head pins. Attach head pins at equal intervals on each side of center beaded eye pin.

6) In same manner, use an assortment of beads to make 37 additional beaded head pins, varying the lengths of head pins. Attach, evenly spaced, on each side of center eye pin. ●

MATERIALS

- Silver bugle beads
- Silver and clear seed beads
- Silver and frosted tube beads
- Assorted beads: spacers, silver, round clear and frosted
- Small and medium silver star charms
- 18 inches silver chain with links and lobster claw clasp
- Silver eye pins
- Silver head pins
- Round-nose pliers
- Chain-nose pliers
- Wire nippers

FINISHED SIZE

18 inches

Warm & Cool

Design by **Vicki Blizzard**

Winter months can be so fickle—some days cool, some warm, with flowers blooming through the snow. This necklace, with warm freshwater pearls, cool blue chalcedony and sterling silver, is a reflection of the season!

INSTRUCTIONS

1) String two crimp beads ½ inch from end of beading wire; place wire end through end of lobster claw and back through both crimp beads. Gently squeeze crimp bead furthest away from clasp and fold in half with crimp pliers.

2) String a sterling silver heishe bead, rice pearl, potato pearl, chalcedony bead, potato pearl, chalcedony bead, potato pearl, chalcedony bead, potato pearl and a rice pearl. Repeat stringing sequence eight more times and string a sterling silver heishe bead.

3) Repeat step 1, stringing closed jump ring instead of lobster claw clasp. ●

Sources: Beading wire from Beadalon.

MATERIALS

- 27 (6mm) round chalcedony beads
- 36 (6 x 8mm) potato-shaped freshwater pearls (drilled sideways)
- 18 (3 x 5mm) rice-shaped freshwater pearls (drilled longways)
- 10 (4mm) sterling silver heishe beads
- 4 (1.5mm) crimp beads
- 1 (4.7mm) sterling silver closed jump ring
- Sterling silver lobster claw clasp
- 25 inches .015-inch-diameter 19-strand nylon-coated flexible beading wire
- Crimp pliers
- Wire nippers

FINISHED SIZE

21 inches

Midnight Sky

Designs by **Katherine McBee**

Triple strands of snowflake obsidian separate and converge in a necklace that looks more complicated than it really is.

Project note: When stringing beads onto each strand, secure remaining strands to a smooth surface with tape.

INSTRUCTIONS

Necklace

1) Hold the three 36-inch lengths of monofilament thread together; string a crimp bead onto one end through all strands approximately ½ inch away from thread ends. Place ends through one half of toggle clasp and back through crimp bead. Gently squeeze crimp bead with crimp tool.

2) Holding all three strands together, string on two Bali spacers, small bead, medium Bali spacer, three large beads and a medium Bali spacer.

3) Separate strands and string three small beads onto each.

4) Hold strands together and string two large beads.

5) Repeat step 3.

6) Repeat step 4.

7) Separate strands and string three chips onto each strand.

8) Repeat step 4.

9) Continue alternating between steps 7 and 4 fourteen times.

10) Repeat step 3.

11) Repeat step 4.

12) Repeat step 3.

13) Join strands together and thread on a medium Bali spacer, three large beads, medium Bali spacer, small bead and two small Bali spacers.

14) Slide on a crimp bead and attach remaining end of toggle clasp in same manner as in step 1.

Bracelet

1) Holding all three 16-inch lengths of clear elastic thread together, string on two large beads.

2) Separate strands and string three chips onto each strand.

3) Continue alternating between steps 1 and 2 until desired length is achieved. End with two large beads.

4) Tie a double knot; secure knot with jeweler's cement. ●

Sources: Crimp tool, crimp tubes and clear elastic from The Beadery; clasp, spacers, chips and round beads from Blue Moon Beads.

MATERIALS

- Small, medium and large snowflake obsidian beads
- Snowflake obsidian chips
- 4 small Bali spacer beads
- 4 medium Bali spacer beads
- 2 silver crimp beads
- Silver-tone heart toggle clasp
- 3 (36-inch) lengths mono-filament thread
- 3 (16-inch) lengths 0.5mm clear elastic thread
- Ruler
- Crimp tool
- Jeweler's cement
- Masking tape

FINISHED SIZES

Necklace
   16½ inches

Bracelet
   Will fit small and large wrists

Arabian Nights

Design by **Vicki Blizzard**

This simply elegant piece is just as at home with a little black dress as it is with a suit. Seed beads serve as spacers and give the look of hand-knotting between the beads, and an extension chain lets you change the length to complement your neckline.

INSTRUCTIONS

1) Cut a 20-inch length of black beading wire. String two crimp beads ½ inch from end of beading wire; place wire end through clasp and thread back through crimp beads. Use crimp pliers to flatten and fold crimp bead furthest away from clasp.

2) String a seed bead, a cube bead, a seed bead, a bicone bead, a seed bead, a cube bead, a seed bead, a heishe spacer, a round Bali bead and a silver spacer. Repeat stringing sequence eight additional times. String a seed bead, a cube bead, a seed bead, a bicone bead, a seed bead, a cube bead and a seed bead.

3) String two crimp beads and last link of chain. Thread end of wire back through crimp beads and several other beads. Use crimp pliers to flatten and fold crimp bead furthest away from chain.

4) On a head pin, thread a seed bead and a cube bead. Use round-nose pliers to form a wrapped loop with head pin, inserting other end of chain into loop before wrapping. Trim excess head pin. ●

Source: Beading wire and crimp beads from Beadalon.

MATERIALS

- 21 (7mm) red coral diagonally-drilled cube beads
- 10 (5mm) silver corrugated bicone beads
- 9 (10mm) silver round Bali beads
- 18 (8mm) silver heishe spacer beads
- 41 black seed beads
- 9mm silver lobster claw clasp
- 4⅛-inch length of silver chain with 3mm links
- 2-inch silver Bali head pin
- 4 black crimp beads
- 32 inches .015-inch-diameter 49-strand black nylon-coated flexible beading wire
- Chain-nose pliers
- Round-nose pliers
- Crimp pliers
- Wire nippers

FINISHED SIZE

17½ inches with a 4¼-inch extender

Pearl Elegance

Designs by **Vicki Blizzard**

Indulge yourself with three times the elegance of fiery lead crystals mingled with freshwater pearls with this triple-strand necklace and coordinating earrings!

INSTRUCTIONS

Necklace

Strand 1 (top strand)

1) Cut a 24-inch-length of beading wire. String two crimp beads 1 inch from end of beading wire; place end through top ring of filigree part of clasp and back through two crimp beads. Use crimp pliers to squeeze first crimp bead (furthest away from clasp) and fold it in half.

2) String 15 pearls onto wire; string a round Austrian crystal bead, a rondelle, a second round crystal bead, a rondelle, a third round crystal bead, a rondelle and a fourth round crystal bead (crystal-bead unit) onto wire. String 20 pearls, a crystal-bead unit, 20 pearls, a crystal-bead unit and 15 pearls onto wire.

3) String 2 crimp beads and top ring of insert part of clasp onto wire. Fold wire back through two crimp beads and pull securely to tighten necklace. Squeeze and fold crimp bead (furthest away from clasp) with crimp pliers. Trim excess wire.

Strand 2 (middle strand)

1) Repeat Step 1 of Strand 1, cutting a 30-inch-length of wire and using center ring of clasp.

2) String onto wire 25 pearls, a crystal-bead unit, 7 pearls, a crystal-bead unit, 9 pearls, a crystal-bead unit, 7 pearls, a crystal-bead unit and 25 pearls.

3) Repeat Step 3 of Strand 1, using center ring of clasp.

Strand 3 (bottom strand)

1) Repeat Step 1 of Strand 1, cutting a 34-inch-length of wire and using bottom ring of clasp.

2) String onto wire 8 pearls, a crystal-bead unit, 20 pearls, a crystal-bead unit, 25 pearls, a crystal-bead unit, 20 pearls, a crystal-bead unit and 8 pearls.

3) Repeat Step 3 of Strand 1, using bottom ring of clasp.

Earrings

1) Thread a round crystal, a rondelle and a round crystal onto a head pin. Use round-nose pliers to make a loop. Before closing loop attach to ear wire. Close loop by wrapping excess wire around loop's base; trim. (See Bead Basics on page 95)

2) Repeat Step 1 for second earring. ●

Sources: Pearls, Swarovski crystals, rondelles, clasp, crimp beads and ear wires from Fire Mountain Gems & Beads; beading wire from Beadalon.

MATERIALS

- 3 (16-inch) strands of 4mm rice freshwater pearls
- 48 (6mm) Sian round Austrian crystals
- 35 (6mm) gold rondelles with red rhinestones
- Gold-filled triple-strand filigree clasp
- 12 (2mm) gold crimp beads
- 2 gold ear wires
- 2 gold head pins
- 88 inches 19-strand (.018mm) nylon-coated flexible beading wire
- Round-nose pliers
- Chain-mail pliers
- Crimp pliers
- Wire nippers

FINISHED SIZES

Necklace

17 inches

Earrings

1 inch long

Crystal Elegance

Design by **Kelly Hempton**, courtesy of Art & Soul Beads

Glitter and sparkle your way through any occasion with this work of art created with dazzling crystal beads. For added flair, make a coordinating bracelet.

MATERIALS

11 (20mm x 8mm) clear elongated diamond-shaped Swarovski crystal beads

19 (10mm x 12mm x 5mm) clear faceted diamond-shaped rock crystal beads

6 (8mm) clear diagonally-drilled Swarovski crystal cube beads

20 (5mm) clear Swarovski crystal saucer beads

36 (3mm) sterling silver large-hole round beads

22 (2mm) sterling silver round beads

22 Bali bead caps

2 (1mm x 1mm) sterling silver crimp beads

11 (2-inch) sterling silver head pins

Sterling silver and crystal toggle clasp

22 inches .015-inch-diameter 3-strand stringing cable

Flush cutters

Crimp pliers

Round-nose pliers

FINISHED SIZE

16¼ inches long

INSTRUCTIONS

1) For beaded dangles, slide the following sequence onto a 2-inch head pin: a 2mm sterling silver bead, a Bali bead cap, a Swarovski elongated diamond-shaped crystal, a Bali bead cap and a 2mm sterling silver bead. Repeat to make eleven dangles. Use round-nose pliers to form a wrapped head pin loop at top of ten of the dangles; trim excess wire.

2) Slide a crimp bead 2 inches from one end of cable; thread end through one half of toggle clasp and back through crimp bead. Gently squeeze crimp bead with crimp pliers. String on a 3mm large-hole round bead to conceal crimp.

3) String on a faceted diamond-shaped crystal and a 3mm large-hole round bead; repeat six additional times.

4) String the following sequence: a diagonally-drilled cube, a 3mm large-hole round bead, a crystal saucer, a beaded dangle, a crystal saucer, a 3mm large-hole round bead, a faceted diamond-shaped bead, a 3mm large-hole round bead, a crystal saucer, a beaded dangle, a crystal saucer and a 3mm large-hole round bead. Repeat sequence four additional times.

5) String on a diagonally-drilled cube; repeat step 3, only in reverse.

6) String on a 3mm large-hole round bead, crimp bead and remaining half of clasp; thread cable end back through crimp bead. Pull beads tightly into place and keep end tight. Gently squeeze crimp bead; slide 3mm large-hole round bead over crimp to conceal. Trim excess wire.

7) Form a wrapped head pin loop on top of remaining beaded dangle, attaching loop to one end of clasp before wrapping. ●

Source: Swarovski crystal beads, silver beads and toggle clasp from Art & Soul Beads.

Shades of Blue

Design by **Katie Hacker**

MATERIALS

4mm to 8mm blue, purple
and gray glass beads in
assorted shapes

88 (5mm) silver bugle beads

84 (11/0) purple seed beads

5 (10mm) silver leaf beads

2 (6mm) silver rondelle beads

4 purple E beads

5 (6mm) silver jump rings

25 (2-inch) silver head pins

4 silver crimp tubes

Antique silver toggle clasp

5-inch antique silver charm
bracelet chain

4 (8-inch) lengths .015-inch-
diameter 19-strand nylon-
coated flexible beading wire

Wire nippers

Crimp pliers

Round-nose pliers

Chain-nose pliers

FINISHED SIZE

17½ inches

Charms aren't just for bracelets! Make your own beaded charms and attach them to a section of chain to create the focal area for this snazzy necklace. Add purchased metal charms for stylish texture and shine.

INSTRUCTIONS

1) Slide desired bead or beads onto a head pin; use round-nose pliers to form a wrapped head pin loop at top, attaching loop to a link in chain before wrapping. Trim excess wire. Repeat for all head pins.

2) Slide each leaf bead onto a jump ring; attach jump rings, evenly spaced, onto chain.

3) Hold two pieces of beading wire together; string a crimp tube 1 inch from one end on both wires. Thread wire ends through last link on chain and back through crimp tube. Gently squeeze and fold crimp tube in half with crimp pliers.

4) Hold wires together and string on a 6mm silver rondelle bead and a purple E bead. Separate strands and beginning with a bugle bead, string 22 bugle beads and 21 seed beads onto each strand, alternating bugle and seed beads. Hold strands together and string on a purple E bead, a crimp tube and one half of toggle clasp. Thread wire ends back through crimp tube and E bead. Gently squeeze and fold crimp tube in half. Trim excess wire.

5) Repeat steps 3 and 4 for other half of necklace, attaching remaining half of toggle clasp. ●

Sources: Beads and toggle clasp from Blue Moon Beads; beading wire and crimp tubes from Beadalon.

Shades of Purple

Designs by **Vicki Blizzard**

Iridescent lavender seed beads form a delicate chain on either side of sparkling focus beads.

INSTRUCTIONS

Necklace

1) Cut a 20-inch length of beading wire. String two crimp beads ½ inch from end of wire; place wire end through clasp and back through crimp beads. Use chain-nose pliers to flatten crimp bead furthest away from clasp.

2) String 7 inches of seed beads.

3) String 4mm cube, rondelle, 6mm cube, rondelle, rectangular bead, rondelle, 6mm cube, rondelle and 4mm cube onto wire.

4) String 7 inches of seed beads.

5) String two crimp beads and jump ring. Thread end of wire back through crimp beads. Use chain-nose pliers to flatten crimp bead furthest away from jump ring.

Bracelet

1) Follow steps 1–5 of necklace, cutting a 12-inch length of beading wire and stringing 2⅛ inches of seed beads.

Earrings

1) String a rondelle and rectangular bead onto an eye pin with three holes. Use round-nose pliers to form a wrapped loop at top, attaching it to ear wire before wrapping. Trim excess wire.

2) String a seed bead and a 6mm cube onto a head pin; form a loop at top and trim excess wire. Open loop and attach to center hole in eye pin; close loop.

3) String a seed bead and a 4mm cube onto a head pin; repeat once. Attach head pins to remaining holes on eye pin in same manner as in step 2.

4) Repeat steps 1–3 for remaining ear wire. ●

Source: Beading wire from Beadalon.

MATERIALS

- 4 (25 x 12mm) iridescent purple flat engraved rectangular glass beads
- 6 (6mm) amethyst Swarovski crystal cube beads
- 8 (4mm) amethyst Swarovski crystal cube beads
- 10 (4mm) amethyst and silver Swarovski crystal rondelle beads
- Approximately 300 iridescent purple seed beads
- 2 (9mm) sterling silver lobster claw clasps
- 2 (4.7mm) sterling silver closed jump rings
- Sterling silver ear wires
- 8 (1.5mm) sterling silver crimp beads
- 6 sterling silver head pins
- 2 sterling silver eye pins with 3 holes
- 32 inches .015-inch-diameter 49-strand nylon-coated flexible beading wire
- Round-nose pliers
- Chain-nose pliers
- Wire nippers

FINISHED SIZES

Necklace
  16½ inches

Bracelet
  7 inches

Earrings
  2½ inches long

Belt Loop Chains

Designs by **Margot Potter**

Who needs a belt? Stylish beaded dangles
will be your jeans' new best friends!

INSTRUCTIONS

Happy Cat Chain

1) Use chain- and round-nose pliers to open the end links of the Figaro chain and attach them to the small toggle clasp.

2) On an eye pin, thread a red glass rondelle, metal accent, cat charm, metal accent and a red glass rondelle; use round-nose pliers to create a loop above top rondelle. Attach eye pin to toggle clasp; trim excess wire.

3) Attach three cloisonné fish charms to bottom of eye pin.

Peachy-Keen Chain

1) Attach medium curb chain to a large toggle clasp in same manner as in step 1 of Happy Cat Chain.

2) On an eye pin, thread the pink glass round bead and the glass leaf bead; create a wrapped head pin loop above glass leaf, attaching to another eye pin before wrapping. ***Note:*** *Take care when wrapping the wire above the glass leaf as tension from the wire can cause the leaf to break.*

3) Thread pink floral and multicolor floral beads onto the attached eye pin; create a loop at top and attach to toggle clasp.

Elegant Deco Chain

1) Use side cutters to cut elongated cable chain into three pieces measuring 5 inches, 2 inches and 1½ inches.

2) Attach 5-inch piece to large toggle clasp in same manner as in step 1 of Happy Cat Chain; attach remaining lengths to the large round toggle clasp end.

3) Thread a red disc, hemalyke rondelle and a black faceted bead onto an eye pin; create a loop above top bead. Trim excess wire.

4) Repeat step 3.

5) Attach a small round toggle clasp end to the bottom of each eye pin; attach eye pins to ends of chains. ●

Source: Chains and toggle clasps from Beadalon.

MATERIALS

- Silver chain: 8½ inches elongated cable, 6 inches medium curb and 5⅞ inches Figaro
- 3 silver toggle clasps: 2 large and 1 small
- 2 silver small round toggle clasp ends
- 4 silver eye pins
- 1 silver head pin
- 2 red onyx flat discs
- 2 (4mm) black faceted glass beads
- 2 hemalyke rondelles
- 2 red glass rondelles
- 2 flat metal accent beads
- Carved bone cat head charm
- 3 small cloisonné fish charms
- Chinese lamp work pink floral bead
- Chinese blown glass multicolor floral bead
- 6mm Czech glass pink A/B round bead
- Mint green flat glass leaf bead
- Round-nose pliers
- Chain-nose pliers
- Side cutters

FINISHED SIZE

5 to 6¼ inches

Asian Style

Designs by **Vicki Blizzard**

Add a touch of mystery and intrigue to your wardrobe with lightweight, oriental-influenced acrylic beads in warm shades of red!

MATERIALS

2 large red flat faceted beads

8 large red chunky red beads

15 medium red chunky beads

12 small red chunky beads

8 (6mm x 10mm) red diamond beads

41 (6mm) red round beads

133 (4mm x 6mm) red bicone beads

40 mm donut pendant

3 (2mm) silver crimp beads

2-inch silver head pins

Heavy silver toggle clasp

66 inches 49-strand (.018mm) nylon-coated flexible beading wire

14 inches stretch cord

Round-nose pliers

Chain-mail pliers

Crimp pliers

Wire nippers

Jeweler's cement

FINISHED SIZES

Necklace

18 inches

Bracelet

3 inches in diameter

INSTRUCTIONS

Necklace

Pendant dangle

1) Cut a 6-inch length of beading wire. String 35 bicone beads on wire. String crimp bead on wire. Thread opposite end of wire through crimp bead. Pull both ends of wire to shape beads into a circle; crimp the crimp bead.

2) Thread a bicone bead, a round bead and a flat faceted bead onto head pin; set aside. Attach beaded circle through center of donut pendant with a lark's head knot, positioning crimp bead so that it is behind donut and not visible from front. Form a loop at top of head pin, attaching head pin to bottom loop of circle of beads before closing.

Necklace

1) Cut remaining wire in half. String 35 bicone beads on both strands of wire, centering beads. Attach beads to pendant with a lark's head knot through donut. Thread all ends of wire through the remaining flat faceted bead.

2) Separate wires into two groups of two wires and string one side of necklace as follows: 2 bicone beads, large chunky bead, medium chunky bead, 3 large chunky beads, 4 medium chunky beads. Separate wires again. *On one strand, string 7 bicone beads; on the other strand string 3 small chunky beads. Thread both wire strands through a diamond bead. Separate strands. On one strand string 7 bicone beads; on the other stand string 5 round beads. Thread both strands through a diamond bead. Repeat stringing sequence from *.

3) Thread both strands of wire through 5 round beads, a crimp bead, a bicone bead and the toggle clasp. Thread ends back through the bicone bead, the crimp bead and several round beads. Pull ends and crimp the crimp bead. Trim wire ends. Repeat stringing sequence on other half of necklace.

Bracelet

1) String remaining medium chunky beads and round beads on stretch cord, alternating beads.

2) Tie ends of cord in a square knot. Dot ends of cord with jeweler's glue; let dry. Trim ends. ●

Sources: Assorted Elements Beads and pendant from the Beadery; beading wire from Beadalon, GS Hypo Cement Germanow-Simon Corp.

Red-Hot Twisted Choker

Design by **Vicki Blizzard**

This necklace can be worn in many of ways: Wear it twisted or wear strands unlatched and knotted at the end; wear strands individually or wear them in groups. You decide—this is never the same necklace twice!

INSTRUCTIONS

1) For each strand, cut a 100-inch-length of nylon and thread through a beading needle. Pull nylon until ends are even; hold ends together and tie in a secure knot.

2) Create individual strands as specified below or as desired.

Strand 1: Alternate red bugle beads and rainbow ruby red bugle beads for 42 inches.

Strand 2: Thread 21 inches of red triangle beads and 21 inches of red rainbow triangle beads.

Strand 3: Thread 21 inches of matte red cube beads and 21 inches of red-lined clear cube beads.

Strand 4: Thread 21 inches of rainbow ruby red seed beads and 21 inches of silver-lined ruby red seed beads.

Strand 5: Thread 10 transparent rainbow strawberry delica beads and 1 Sian Austrian crystal bead. Repeat until 42 inches are threaded.

Strand 6: Thread 21 inches of metallic raspberry hex delica beads and 21 inches of cherry-lined clear delica beads.

Strand 7: Thread 21 inches of opaque matte dark red delica beads and 21 inches of translucent orange/red delica beads.

3) After strand is beaded, bring beginning and ending thread ends together, knot securely and dot knot with a drop of jewelry cement. When cement is dry, trim ends.

4) To wear as a twisted choker, loop one end of all strands over opened clasp. Loop other ends of strands over one finger and twist several times. Wrap twisted strands around neck, place clasp through ends around finger and close. ●

Sources: Beads, clasp, thread and needles from Fire Mountain Gems & Beads; GS Hypo Cement from Germanow-Simon Corp.

MATERIALS

- Various packages of beads in assorted sizes, colors and shapes (Model uses five shades of delica beads, two shades of seed beads, two types of cube beads, two types of triangle beads, two shades of bugle beads and 3mm Sian Austrian crystal bicone beads.)
- Red size 00 nylon thread
- Medium sterling silver twister clasp
- Beading needles
- Jewelry cement

FINISHED SIZE

24 inches (each strand, untwisted)

MATERIALS

Wooden disks: 2 (1-inch) and
    1 (1½-inch)

4 x 6-inch soft copper
    embossing sheet

3 small self-adhesive clear
    dimensional circles

Decorative circle and clock
    rubber stamps

Clear embossing ink pad

Black metal stamp ink pad

Clear and gold embossing
    powders

Black chisel-tip permanent
    marker

Metallic gold wax finish

Gloss lacquer

18-gauge black copper wire

2.5mm black rubber tubing

8 (6mm) antique large-hole
    gold spacers

8 aged bone disks

2 gold spring cord ends

2 (6mm) gold jump rings

12mm gold lobster clasp

2 earring wires

Metal baking tray

Soft cloth

Scrap paper

Rubber gloves

Embossing heat tool

Stylus tool set (includes 2
    wooden and 1 metal-tipped)

Nylon-jaw pliers

Combo pliers

5½ x 4½-inch double-sided
    adhesive

2-part epoxy glue

FINISHED SIZES

Necklace

    23 inches

Earrings

    2⅞ inches long

Treasures of Antiquity

Designs by **Lisa Galvin**

Metal has fascinated artisans for centuries. This stunning jewelry set was inspired by the designer's interest in history and archeology. With a few widely available materials, you can create a modern treasure of your own.

INSTRUCTIONS

1) Trace a 1-inch disk and a 1½-inch disk onto scrap paper to create patterns for both sizes. Color edges of all wooden disks and a ¼-inch border on reverse sides with permanent marker.

2) Using patterns, cut two pieces of double-sided adhesive and copper for each wooden disk. Set wooden disks and adhesive aside.

3) Place copper pieces onto metal baking sheet; use embossing heat tool to heat treat copper. To heat treat, start in a small area and move heat tool slowly as temperature of copper rises. The metal finish will change, creating a varied color appearance. Let copper pieces cool completely.

4) Place heat-treated copper circles onto scrap paper and stamp desired images onto reverse sides with black metal stamp ink pad; heat set images. Apply clear embossing powder to each circle and emboss.

5) Use the precut double-sided adhesive circles to attach stamped copper pieces to the reverse sides of matching size wooden disks. Smooth copper with finger to remove air bubbles. Use metal-tipped embossing stylus to emboss tiny dots or swirls onto the copper sections that aren't stamped.

6) Turn disks over to front side. Attach a self-adhesive clear dimensional circle to each disk. Press a double-sided adhesive circle onto each wooden disk. Smooth adhesive with wooden stylus to remove air bubbles before removing top cover sheet on adhesive.

7) Cut a few small pieces of black copper wire; use round-nose pliers to form wires into various swirl and zigzag shapes. Place wire shapes on top of adhesive on disks.

8) Align remaining copper circles with edges of disks and press to attach, covering dimensional circles and wire shapes. Once copper circles are secure, use metal-tipped embossing stylus to carefully push metal, filling in shapes. Emboss swirls and tiny dots on flat portions of disks.

9) Wearing rubber gloves, use a soft cloth to apply wax finish to both sides of each coin. Let wax set for approximately three minutes before buffing; remove excess wax while leaving a small amount of wax in grooves of disks creating an aged effect. Let dry.

10) Use metal-tipped stylus to create small slash marks around outer edges on each disk. Roll edges into embossing ink pad and emboss edges with gold embossing powder. Repeat as needed for desired effect.

Note: *Do not allow metal to become too hot as it can affect the adhesive underneath copper.*

11) Cut a 2¾ to 3½-inch piece of 18-gauge black wire; fold in half around tip of round-nose pliers.

Use nylon-jaw pliers to form ends into swirls. Hold folded loop with round-nose pliers and wrap wire around itself twice, forming a top loop. Use 2-part epoxy to glue swirls to front and back of a disk.

Repeat for each disk. Set disks aside to allow glue to cure.

12) Brush each disk with lacquer; insert a piece of wire through top loop on each disk and hang disks to dry for 20 minutes. Reapply lacquer if a heavier coat is desired.

13) For necklace, cut a 22-inch length of rubber tubing; attach one spring cord end to one end of tubing with 2-part epoxy. Flatten last ring on spring end to fasten.

14) Slide beads onto tubing in the following order: a spacer bead, two aged bone disks, a spacer bead, a large copper coin, a spacer bead, two aged bone disks and a spacer bead.

15) Attach spring cord end to remaining end of tubing in same manner as in step 13. Attach a jump ring onto each cord end; attach lobster claw clasp to one jump ring.

16) For earrings, cut a 4-inch length of 18-gauge black wire. Use round-nose pliers to form a loop at one end; slip loop onto earring wire before closing loop.

17) Slide a spacer bead, two aged bone disks and another spacer bead onto wire; trim wire end ½ inch from last bead. Form another loop below last bead, attaching loop to a small copper coin loop before closing.

18) Repeat steps 16 and 17 for second earring. ●

Cotton Candy

Designs by **Vicki Blizzard**

Delicate shades of pink and tiny silver leaves shout romance in a sophisticated manner. Wear the unique leaf clasp on the side for maximum style impact!

INSTRUCTIONS

Strand 1

1) Cut a 23-inch piece of beading wire. String two crimp beads ½ inch from end of beading wire; place wire end through jump ring and back through both crimp beads. Gently squeeze crimp bead furthest away from ring and fold in half with crimp pliers.

2) Alternate stringing a silver-lined pink seed bead and a pink rice pearl, ending with a silver-lined pink seed bead. Strand should measure approximately 17 inches long.

3) Repeat step 1; trim excess wire.

Strand 2

1) Repeat step 1 of Strand 1.

2) Alternate stringing a silver-lined pink E bead and a medium rose or mauve glass bead, ending with a silver-lined pink E bead. Strand should measure approximately 17 inches long.

3) Repeat step 3 of Strand 1.

Strand 3

1) Repeat step 1 of Strand 1.

2) String a frosted round bead, a leaf bead and a frosted round bead (leaf unit); string three pink glass beads; string a leaf unit; string three pink glass beads; string a leaf unit; string five pink flat chip-type beads;

MATERIALS

- Approximately 34 assorted medium mauve and rose glass beads
- Approximately 33 assorted medium-to-large pink glass beads, including flat chip-type beads and a 1-inch focus bead
- 22 (5mm) frosted pink round beads
- 68 pink rice pearls
- 35 silver-lined pink E beads
- 69 silver-lined pink seed beads
- 40 pale pink seed beads
- 11 silver leaf beads
- 2 silver leaf cones
- Silver long-leaf toggle clasp
- 6 (4mm) silver jump rings
- 14 silver crimp beads
- 85 inches .015-inch-diameter 49-strand nylon-coated flexible beading wire
- Crimp pliers
- Wire nippers

FINISHED SIZE

21 inches (including clasp)

string a leaf unit; string three pink glass beads; string a leaf unit; string three pink glass beads with 1-inch focus bead in center; string a leaf unit; string three pink glass beads; string a leaf unit; string three pink glass beads; string a leaf unit; string five pink chip-type beads; string a leaf unit; string three pink glass beads; string a leaf unit; string three pink glass beads; string a leaf unit.

3) Repeat step 3 of Strand 1.

Attach cone & clasp

1) Cut an 8-inch piece of beading wire. Thread 10 pale pink seed beads, one end of toggle clasp and 10 pale pink seed beads onto beading wire. Slide all beads to center of wire.

2) Thread both ends of wire through narrow end of leaf cone.

3) Thread one end of wire through jump rings on one end of each strand of necklace. Thread crimp bead onto wire. Insert other end of wire from opposite end of crimp bead. Pull both ends until jump rings are pulled into wide end of cone. Close the crimp bead securely and trim wire ends.

4) Repeat steps 1 and 2 to attach remaining end of clasp. ●

Source: Lampwork and Czech bead mixes, pearls, cones and toggle from Blue Moon Beads; beading wire from Beadalon.

Gossamer Moonlight

Design by **Margot Potter**

Softer than a whisper, this iridescent choker simply floats on your neck. Light enough to wear with an elegant evening gown, it will also look pretty with your favorite cold-weather shrug!

MATERIALS

1⅞-inch-diameter 2-hole
  mother-of-pearl button
4 (2mm) blue-lined Czech
  glass faceted ovals
3 freshwater green
  potato pearls
3 (½-inch-long) 24-gauge
  sterling silver head pins
4 (½-inch-long) 22-gauge
  sterling silver head pins
18-gauge large sterling silver
  jump ring
26 inches ¼-inch-wide sheer
  blue ribbon
26 inches ¼-inch-wide sheer
  olive green ribbon
26 inches 1.5mm diameter
  black leather cord
Wire nippers
Round-nose pliers
Chain-nose pliers
Jeweler's cement

FINISHED SIZE

Can be worn to fit any neck size

INSTRUCTIONS

1) Use round-nose pliers to open jump ring and thread it through the front holes of button. Close jump ring. Thread ribbons through buttonhole from back to front, making sure there is an even length on each side. Thread the four ribbon ends back through the ribbon loop formed in back; slide loop flush to the top of the button.

2) Thread the leather cord halfway through the jump ring extending on back of button. Take one half of cord and knot it around one set of ribbon pairs at the top of the button. Repeat for other half of cord.

3) Slide a blue-lined faceted oval onto a 22-gauge head pin; use round-nose pliers to form a loop above oval. Trim excess wire. Repeat for remaining blue-lined faceted ovals.

4) Slide a green potato pearl onto a 24-gauge head pin; use round-nose pliers to form a loop above pearl. Trim excess wire. Repeat for remaining potato pearls.

5) Attach beaded head pins to jump ring on front of button, alternating ovals and pearls from right to left. Secure loops closed with chain-nose pliers.

6) Use fingers to tug along lengths of ribbon to create a distressed effect; apply a small amount of jeweler's cement on ribbon ends to prevent fraying. To wear necklace, tie in a bow around neck. ●

Sources: Potato pearls from Thunderbird Supply Co.; GS Hypo Cement from Germanow-Simon Corp.

Shimmering Pearls

CONTINUED FROM PAGE 15

Strand 3

1) Cut a 22-inch length of beading wire. String two crimp beads and 13 seed beads ½ inch from end of beading wire; thread wire end through jump ring on clasp and back through the crimp beads and seed beads. Tug wire gently until loop closes around jump ring. Gently squeeze crimp bead furthest away from jump ring and fold in half with crimp pliers.

2) String a small rice pearl, a daisy spacer, a small rice pearl and 13 seed beads. Repeat beading sequence 15 additional times.

3) Repeat step 3 of Strand 1, pulling wire back through crimp beads and 13 seed beads before closing crimp beads. ●

Source: Beading wire from Beadalon.

Metallic Treasures

CONTINUED FROM PAGE 80

Earrings

1) Thread a round metallic bead onto a decorative head pin; use round-nose pliers to form a loop above bead.

2) Attach loop to copper earring finding. Close loop and trim excess wire.

3) Repeat steps 1 and 2 for remaining earring. ●

Source: Crimp tool from The Beadery; clasp, copper spacers, beads, earring findings and crimp beads from Blue Moon Beads.

Beads & Bubbles

CONTINUED FROM PAGE 40

11) Tie another knot ¾ inch from last knot and string on the following: seed bead, three small aqua beads, two medium aqua beads, small aqua bead, hammered flat bead, small aqua bead, two medium aqua beads, three small aqua beads and a seed bead. Tie a knot.

12) Repeat step 8.

13) Repeat step 4 to end strand and to attach ends to bottom loops on 3-strand findings.

14) Open two jump rings and slide one on each necklace end; attach lobster claw clasp to one jump ring. Close jump rings with chain-nose pliers. ●

Sources: Silk beading cord and thread conditioner from Beadalon; aqua beads and mother-of-pearl nuggets from The Beadery.

Copper Canyon

CONTINUED FROM PAGE 86

8) Repeat step 6, attaching second 18-inch length to clasp on the outside of the first strand.

9) String the following onto wire: African green rectangle, bronze pearl, khaki pearl head pin, bronze pearl, African green rectangle, bronze pearl, copper charm and bronze pearl. Repeat three times. String an African green rectangle and a bronze pearl. String on beaded pietersite rectangle eye pin.

10) Repeat beading sequence in step 9, only in reverse.

11) String on a crimp tube; place wire end through remaining half of clasp and back through crimp tube. Crimp the crimp tube. Trim excess wire. ●

Sources: Green jasper rectangles from Thunderbird Supply Co.; pietersite rectangle and copper head pins from Great Craft Works; rondelles and pearls from JS Beads; clasp and copper charms from Blue Moon Beads; beading wire and findings from Beadalon.

Bead Basics

Creating your own beaded jewelry is easy and only takes a few tools. Practice these techniques on less-expensive metal findings. Once your finishing techniques are perfected, use real sterling silver or vermeil (24k gold plating over sterling silver) to add elegance.

Sizing
Specific sizes for finished pieces are listed. Adjust wire length and add or subtract beads to suit personal preferences.

Photo 1

Photo 2

Photo 3

Crimps
1) String a crimp bead onto wire or thread. Insert wire through optional bead and end of clasp. Optional bead prevents excess friction on crimp bead and will help prevent fraying of beading wire. Thread wire back through optional bead and crimp bead (Photo 1).

2) Hold the crimp bead in the "C" section of crimp pliers. Apply gentle pressure to squeeze and flatten the crimp bead (Photos 2 and 3).

3) Place flattened crimp in the rounding section of crimp pliers. Apply gentle pressure to fold crimp bead in half (Photos 4 and 5).

Photo 4

Photo 5

Jump Rings
1) Open jump rings using two pairs of pliers. Instead of pulling ends of the ring away from each other, slide the ring open by pulling ends in opposite directions (Photo 1).

2) Insert ring through clasp or beaded pin (Photo 2).

3) Close ring by bending ends back toward each other (Photo 3).

Photo 1

Photo 2

Photo 3

Head Pin Loop

1) Thread desired beads onto head or eye pin. Bend the wire at top of pin to form a 45-degree angle. Trim wire approximately ⅜ inch (10mm) from fold (Photo 1). *Note: For consistent trimming, insert a 10mm bead onto wire before trimming and trim flush with bead; remove bead.*

2) Roll end of wire halfway around one prong of round-nose pliers (Photo 2). Release wire.

3) Pick up wire and continue rolling until complete circle is formed flush against last bead on wire (Photo 3).

Photo 1

Photo 2

Photo 3

Wrapped Head Pin Loop

1) Repeat steps 1–3 of Head Pin Loop without trimming wire as noted in step 1.

2) Hold loop with end of wire at bottom of pliers (Photo 1). Use fingers or chain-nose pliers to twist the wire end around beaded wire (Photo 2). Make as many wraps as desired.

3) Trim excess wire and squeeze end gently with pliers to close the wrap (Photo 3).

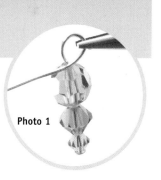

Photo 1

Photo 2

Photo 3

Handy Tools

Crimping Pliers
Squeezes crimp beads and tubes to secure beading wire. The forward "C" section of plier jaws is useful for folding the crimped bead to create a rounded shape and a more finished appearance.

Round-Nose Pliers
The rounded jaws of these pliers are useful for creating loops on beaded head and eye pins.

Wire-Looping Pliers
A graduating round jaw creates loop in three sizes. The concave jaw gently coaxes difficult wire into loops. These are must-have pliers!

Memory Wire Shears
Because memory wire is harder than beading wire or craft wire, it will damage regular wire nippers or scissors. These heavy-duty shears easily cut through memory wire and leave a clean end.

Chain-Nose Pliers
The most versatile pliers, these are useful for everything from bending eye pins to flattening crimps. They are also useful to pick up tiny beads and jump rings that are difficult to grip.

Designer & Project Index

Buyer's Guide

A World of Good Inc., (301) 587-0871, www.aworldofgood.com
Adhesive Products Inc., (510) 526-7616, www.crafterspick.com
American Art Clay Co. Inc., (317) 244-6871, www.amaco.com
Art & Soul Beads, (812) 285-0000, www.artandsoulbeads.com
Artistic Wire Ltd., (630) 530-7567, www.artisticwire.com
Beacon Adhesives Inc., (914) 699-3400, www.beaconcreates.com
Beadalon, (866) 4BEADALON, www.beadalon.com
The Beadery, (401) 539-2432, www.thebeadery.com
Beads & Rocks, (757) 428-9824, www.beadsandrocks.com
Bead Warehouse, (301) 565-0487, www.thebeadwarehouse.com
Blue Moon Beads, (800) 377-6715, www.bluemoonbeads.com
Cousin Corp. of America, (800) 366-2687, www.cousin.com
Darice Inc., (866) 432-7423, www.darice.com
Duncan Enterprises, (800) 438-6226, www.duncancrafts.com
Enchanting Beads, www.enchantingbeads.com
Expo International Inc., (800) 542-4367, www.expointl.com
Fire Mountain Gems & Beads, (800) 423-2319, www.firemountaingems.com
Germanow-Simon Corp., (800) 295-3050, www.gssupplies.com
Great Craft Works, (888) 811-5773, www.greatcraftworks.com
Halcraft USA Inc., (212) 376-1580, www.halcraft.com
Hirschberg Schutz & Co. Inc., (908) 810-1111
Imagine it..., P.O. Box 504, Washington, NY, 10992
JS Beads, www.jsbeads.com
JudiKins, (310) 515-1115, www.judikins.com
Li'l Davis Designs, www.lildavisdesigns.com
Magenta, (800) 565-5254, www.magentarubberstamps.com
Nicole Crafts, www.nicolecrafts.com
Paula Radke Dichroics, www.paularadke.com
Phoenix Jewelry & Parts Inc., (212) 278-8688, www.phoenixbeads.com
Pure Allure Inc., (800) 536-6312
Revelations In Stone, (707) 426-5916
Rings & Things, (800) 366-2156, www.rings-things.com
Sulyn Industries Inc., (954) 755-2311, www.sulyn.com
Tandy Leather Co., (800) 433-3201, www.tandyleather.com
Thunderbird Supply Co., (800) 545-7968, www.thunderbirdsupply.com
Westrim Crafts, (800) 727-2727, www.westrimcrafts.com